YOUR BACKYARD
Wildlife GARDEN

HOW TO ATTRACT AND IDENTIFY
WILDLIFE IN YOUR YARD

YOUR BACKYARD
Wildlife GARDEN

HOW TO ATTRACT AND IDENTIFY
WILDLIFE IN YOUR YARD

MARCUS SCHNECK

FOREWORD BY
CRAIG TUFTS

**CHARTWELL
BOOKS, INC.**

A QUANTUM BOOK

Published by Chartwell Books
A Division of Book Sales Inc.
114 Northfield Avenue
Edison, New Jersey 08837
USA

ISBN 0-7858-1261-X

QUMNAG

This book is produced by
Quantum Publishing
6 Blundell Street
London N7 9BH

Printed in Singapore by
Star Standard Industries (Pte) Ltd.

CONTENTS

In the late 1960s and early 1970s, Americans' interest in the wildlife around them began to reawaken. Many thousands of backyard bird-watchers started along the road to ecological responsibility by landscaping to attract birds to their gardens. By the end of the 1970s, avid bird-watchers and millions of bird gardening enthusiasts (perhaps as many as 12 million, according to one U.S. Fish and Wildlife survey) started extending their efforts to other types of wildlife.

In 1973, the National Wildlife Federation introduced its Backyard Wildlife Habitat Program, which certifies people who demonstrate both effort and knowledge in landscaping their property – no matter what the size – for wildlife. The program now has more than 11,000 participants. We continue to encourage, guide, and listen to those citizens who actively make efforts to improve habitats for birds, butterflies, frogs, and other wildlife. Whether they devote their efforts to a town plot or two suburban acres, to a local school or their employer's corporate grounds, more and more people are committed to providing homes for the incredible and fascinating variety of wild creatures and plants with which we share this planet.

Your Backyard Wildlife Garden builds upon the ground swell of interest in this new gardening ethic. Here, in one beautifully illustrated source book, is a new primer for wildlife gardening throughout the United States. For the beginner, Marcus Schneck starts with the basics – find out what you already have and develop a plan. For those of us who have considered ourselves "backyard habitatters" for years, there are wonderful new ideas about wildlife gardening.

If you are especially interested in "niche" wildlife gardening, there is no need to wade into water gardening too deeply by purchasing a special source book. *Your Backyard Wildlife Garden* offers guidelines for creating an aquatic ecosystem so that you can easily make the giant leap from a simple bird bath to a frog pond with its entertaining list of possible inhabitants. Interested in butterfly gardening? *Your Backyard Wildlife Garden* covers the basics of attracting and providing a safe haven for butterflies and their caterpillars. You will find a preview of your most likely butterfly visitors, lists of butterfly- and moth-attracting plants for adult and caterpillar use, and considerations about pesticide use in the butterfly garden.

This book represents a significant way station en route to the land ethic that naturalist Aldo Leopold so eloquently called for many years ago in *A Sand County Almanac*. We now go well beyond putting out seed in order to attract a few types of birds. Pest control no longer means doling out the pesticides, but seeking balance, tolerance, and knowledge. If we can garden for birds, we now find that we can, and perhaps should, garden for toads, for beetles, for spiders, or for prairie grasses. Our wildlife gardens openly invite the wonders of nature to our doorsteps. *Your Backyard Wildlife Garden* is a working person's guide to that wonder. Pick it up, put it down, get to work, and invite wildlife to your garden!

Craig Tufts

Craig Tufts
Director
Urban Wildlife Programs
National Wildlife Federation

The rate at which we're gobbling up open, wild spaces never fails to amaze me. I just don't have the developer's insight into the reasons why we need another shopping center when many shops in an exactly similar shopping center only five or six miles away have stood empty for more than a year. Didn't the woodlot-field environment that previously filled that site with life serve any purpose?

I'm repelled by the replacement of farmlands by row after row of townhouses or new suburban homes, each with their bare and browning patch of grass and two-point-five trees that will reach maturity sometime after the owner's death. More often than not some clever person will tack a name like "Wildlife Circle" or "Nature's Acres" on this man-made scar.

On the other hand, I realize that a growing population, with increasing amounts of disposable cash and an "American dream" as the measure of success, has needs that must be met. People do need someplace to live and shop and recreate and so on. And, when possible, they want those things supplied in a convenient and pleasant location. Development has been, is, and will continue to be the American way.

Open space and the wild things that live there will continue to be the losers in this never-ending progression. Loss of habitat is the number-one threat to wildlife today. As a result we are losing an incredible number of species every year, at a rate previously unmatched in the history of Earth. There are no indications that this loss will be brought into check anytime soon.

But every property owner can lend a hand in this ultimate battle for the survival of life on Earth. Every quarter-acre or half-acre or tiny terrace can be brought to its fullest potential for use by and benefit to wildlife. We don't have to be content with nearly vacant backyards, filled with dying plant life and nearly devoid of animal life.

For those who decide they want something better for their backyards, a much enriched and fulfilled existence awaits. Every wildlife species that receives our help – no matter how lowly – is willing and able to entertain, educate, and amaze us.

This book will help you to discover an entirely new way of looking at your backyard. By the time you finish these pages, tangled brush, tall grass, thick hedgerows, and snags will no longer represent the "eyesores" that you now may see in them. You will see them, and use them, as the beautiful wildlife magnets they are.

Through many years of studying the library's-worth of material that relates either directly or indirectly to the field of backyard habitat development, I have never seen a single-word title that adequately refers to all of us involved in this pursuit. Therefore, throughout the text you will encounter a new word that I have invented for this purpose. That word is "habitatter," and it means one who develops wildlife habitats in his or her backyard. "Habitatting" is the process of developing wildlife habitats in the backyard.

CREATING THE ENVIRONMENT

NEARLY EVERY PROPERTY, ANYWHERE ACROSS NORTH AMERICA, CAN BE TRANSFORMED INTO A NATURAL WONDERLAND FILLED WITH LIFE AND ACTIVITY. PLANTS, NESTING AND ROOSTING BOXES, AND A STEADY SUPPLY OF WATER ARE THE KEY ELEMENTS IN ANY BACKYARD HABITAT. HERE'S HOW TO GET STARTED WITH ALL THREE IN YOUR OWN BACKYARD.

RIGHT: If you have enough space in your backyard, a wildflower meadow is just one of the magical places you might create. On the other hand, even a small patch of native plants all abloom is an accomplishment to be enjoyed. Although commercial seed mixes are available at relatively low prices, you might try gathering your own seed from the nearest vacant lot.

WHAT DO YOU HAVE ALREADY?

THE FIRST STEP TOWARD transforming a backyard into a wildlife habitat is assessing what is already there. If you're completely new to this world of the habitatter, you might be surprised at what your backyard offers without any changes or additions. But, there is no backyard that can't be made better for wildlife.

Start with an overview of your neighborhood. Take an inventory of the general type of habitat in your community. Is it partially wooded with plenty of large, mature trees? Is it a new development with very little vegetation other than grass? Is it a development that borders on agricultural cropland? It will be much easier and more effective to enhance the overall environment that already exists than to create an entirely different type of environment.

This overview should include your assessment of the attitudes of your neighbors and the municipality as a whole toward the local environment. Perhaps there is very strong sentiment, even governmental ordinances, for a very uniform appearance that favors tightly pruned trees and manicured lawns over deviations such as wildflower meadows and brush piles.

You might want to discuss your ideas with your neighbors to determine exactly what will and will not raise objections. Various sections of this book will provide you with ideas on handling any such objections, short of outright antagonism toward all wildlife.

During this initial process you should also note which plant species seem to be doing well throughout the neighborhood and, if possible, what wildlife species frequent the area.

MAP YOUR OWN BACKYARD

Now, narrow your observation to your own backyard. What do you have already? Diagram your yard as it now exists. Use uniform symbols for the various elements: one type of circle for evergreen trees, another for deciduous trees, a third for shrubs, irregular outlines for beds of plants, squares and rectangles for buildings, straight lines for walkways, a "stick-ladder" for stairs, and so forth. The exact symbols are less important than consistent use of the same symbol for similar elements. (The National Wildlife Federation, 1400 16th Street NW, Washington, DC 20036–2266, sells an inexpensive planning kit complete with a template of appropriate symbols for tracing.)

Use graph paper to draw your diagram to the exact scale of your real backyard. Leave nothing out. All existing plants, buildings, walk-

BELOW: If creatures like white-tailed deer are already visiting your backyard, you have a head start toward making your property a real treasure of a habitat. Watch them while they visit to discover what it is about your backyard that is attracting them.

ways, driveways – everything must be shown. If your backyard features distinct changes in elevation, note these as well.

Label every symbol on the diagram with a number and create a key that explains your numbers completely. Use the same number for similar elements. For example, if you used the number 6 to note an oak tree, use number 6 to label all oak trees.

Make several photocopies of your finished diagram for use in the steps that follow.

Next, using one of the photocopies and some highlighter-type markers, map your various uses of the backyard over the symbols of existing plants and structures. For example, the area nearest the house and extending to the fence at the eastern boundary, where the kids and pets play most often, might be shaded in yellow. Another area at the back fence, where the vegetable garden is planted each year, might be shaded in blue. On this map, also shade in trouble spots, such as perennially wet areas, spots where lawn grasses just won't take hold, steep hills, and the like.

NOW BEGIN TO PLAN

With these two maps completed, you're ready to begin planning what you want your backyard habitat to be. This doesn't necessarily mean the end of your vegetable gardening or the loss of the deck. Your map simply enables you to enhance those elements you choose to retain and develop those that you want to add. (The rest of

this book will explain in detail the various elements needed in a backyard habitat and how to develop each. You will need the information in those chapters to proceed beyond this point in your planning.)

Use graph paper to map your backyard and then number each element:

1 sugar maple	7 pool
2 white ash	8 bridge
3 sycamore	9 terrace
4 flowerbeds	10 path
5 shrubs	11 buildings
6 vegetables	

MAPPING YOUR BACKYARD

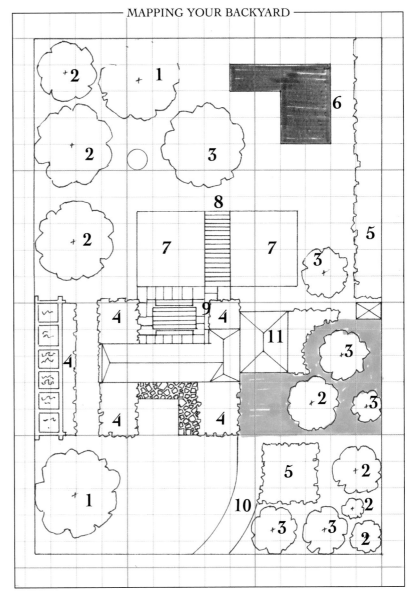

ABOVE: Careful consideration of the plants you already have and forethought about those you want to add are crucial to packing the most benefit into every inch of your backyard habitat. Some plants are of maximum food value because of their blossoms, fruits, and berries. Others are top contenders when it comes to providing shelter and protection. The plants most valuable to wildlife provide both. You may also want to have some plants around just for the colors and textures they offer. Go ahead; follow your own wants.

Plants will be your primary suppliers of food and cover. A diverse selection will produce blooms, fruits, seeds, and nuts at different times of the year, thus providing an adequate supply of food. This same diversity will create a wide range of cover. And, finally, beyond all wildlife benefit, the diversity will bring an array of colors, textures, and scents into the backyard for your enjoyment.

To enhance the natural appearance of the habitat you are creating, forget the row-planting techniques that you employ in the vegetable garden. Plant in clusters or circles. Give plant beds irregular shapes. Create rounded corners instead of square. Scallop some edges as well.

On your photocopied map, in some different color of ink, sketch in these plants. Draw shrubs to the size they will be at maturity and trees to their size when three-quarters grown. This will give you an idea of any conflicts with buildings, driveways, or power lines.

TAMING A SLOPE

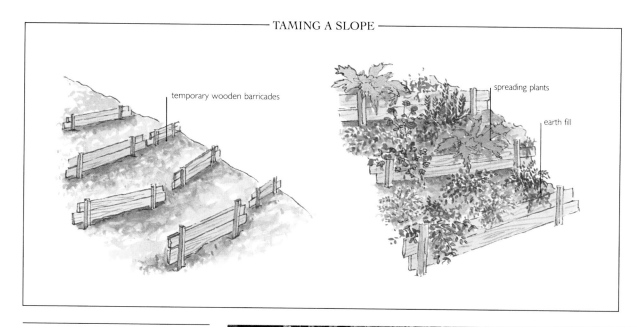

temporary wooden barricades

spreading plants

earth fill

ABOVE: A terrace is a great way to handle erosion while creating a unique environment for wildlife. Fill in behind each barricade, enrich the soil with compost, and plant with spreading plants. When plants are established, you can remove the barricades.

RIGHT: While you want to attract and benefit wildlife as much as possible, you won't want to exclude other uses you enjoy.

Add your water sources, rock or brush piles, bird feeders, and bird houses, and you've just about got your backyard habitat planned. But be sure to leave space for your viewing of the wildlife, both from inside the house and outside. If you garden for vegetables and/or flowers, maintain space for this purpose. And, keep some open lawn for yourself, the kids, and the pets. The overall objective is to make the backyard a more enjoyable place, not a more restrictive one.

DIFFERENT HOMES FOR DIFFERENT RESIDENTS

Habitat, for our purposes, may be defined as that collection of plants, water sources, and terrain that provide wildlife with the three essentials for life – food, water, and cover. This third item includes both shelter from enemies and the elements, and protected places to give birth to and raise the young.

Taking this a bit further, you can see that every species has its own particular definition of optimum habitat. And this definition is distinct from that of all other species.

For example, a cottontail rabbit might spend its entire life – apart from wider-ranging mating forays by males – on an acre of ground. That is, if the acre provides sufficient quantities of grassy and leguminous vegetation to eat and plenty of escape cover, such as thick hedgerows or rock piles. A gray squirrel would have little use for this landscape, opting for another where it would find the nut trees and berry bushes that satisfy its diet and the hollow snags that offer refuge.

A white-tailed deer, on the other hand, will include both of these sites in its overall habitat. But, the deer's lifestyle is based on a much larger home range that might include several home ranges of rabbits and squirrels, in addition to expanses of varying woodland types. In this example, a backyard might provide the entire "world" for a cottontail or two, a major part of the squirrel's living space, and only an occasional stop for the deer.

Diversity of habitat types, therefore, is essential for anyone wanting to attract the maximum number of species into his or her backyard. The rabbit habitat or the squirrel habitat, described earlier, alone might attract two species. But

LEFT, RIGHT and ABOVE: Different species of wildlife make different demands on their environment. Most, however, will adapt their habits to take advantage of special opportunities in the basics of life: shelter, food, and water. The exact spot that a species fills in its environment is known as its *niche*. Species that occupy exactly the same niche compete with one another, but most have slight variations in their needs and wants that allow for co-existence. When you add extra food, water, or shelter to a backyard habitat, you increase the potential for co-existence. The more you add, the more of an impact you can have within some broad limits of the overall environment.

establishing the two distinct habitats within the backyard will likely attract all three.

Of course, this is a very simplified example. Although it is true, it presents a limited vision of what really would transpire. Many other forms of life will be attracted to the "rabbit habitat" or the "squirrel habitat." And others will join the deer in including both the rabbit and squirrel habitats within their territories on occasion.

Wildlife views habitat not only from a map-like horizontal perspective but also for vertical diversity. In this important sense there are actually five zones:

1 underground;
2 ground level, short grasses, and low-lying groundcover;
3 taller grasses, wildflowers, and "weeds;"
4 shrubs and vertical vines;
5 trees.

These different levels are used to varying degrees by the various wildlife species. Some species restrict most of their life activities to one level, while others will use several levels to supply their three basic needs. This is easily seen through the habits of a few common bird species.

The ring-necked pheasant is essentially a ground-based species, feeding, hiding, and nesting at the second and third levels, with occasional food-gathering ventures up into especially fruit-filled shrubs. Juncos and song sparrows are normally ground-based for feeding but seek shelter and nesting sites in

BENEFITS OF A SNAG

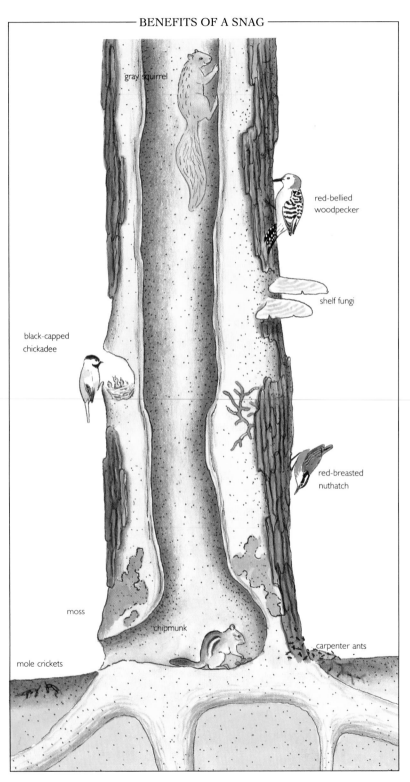

gray squirrel

red-bellied woodpecker

shelf fungi

black-capped chickadee

red-breasted nuthatch

moss

chipmunk

carpenter ants

mole crickets

taller shrubs and in trees. House finches enjoy thick shrub areas and prefer to feed in elevated locations as well. The red-bellied woodpecker spends a great deal of its life in the trees, finding much of its food in the form of insects in the bark and nesting in a tree cavity.

For most backyard habitatters, with limited space to develop, it is best to view these zones as a "hill," slanting upward from the underground level to the tops of the trees. For best viewing of wildlife activity in the habitat you create, the lowest level should be nearest the viewing site and the tree tops should be farthest away.

Habitat diversity must also be considered from a seasonal perspective. Different plants produce their fruits and seeds at different times of the year. A backyard that produces a flurry of food in late summer and early fall will attract a flurry of wildlife visitors at that time. But a backyard planted with a sequential approach will fill much larger portions of the year with crops of fruits and seeds and the accompanying wildlife.

LEFT: A dead or dying mature tree can be a virtual apartment complex and restaurant for wildlife. Such trees are known as *snags* and their existence is encouraged in most modern forestry methods because of their incredible value to wildlife. When such a tree can safely be left standing or secured in the backyard, it will provide a natural magnet for a myriad of wildlife species. Shown here are just a few of the many eastern forest species that would frequent a snag.

RIGHT: Two edges are shown here. The edge in the foreground is where the wildflower field meets and mingles with the lower shrub and vine environment; the one in the background is where the shrubs and vines meet and mingle with the wooded area.

THE CONCEPT OF EDGE

The area where one type of habitat meets and blends for a bit with another type of habitat is known as the edge. Some typical edges occur at the borders of woodland and field, orchards and meadows, open grass and hedgerow, wetlands and fields. This is one of the most critical concepts for anyone who would attract wildlife into the backyard because edges are the most wildlife-filled areas in existence. Species normally found in both types of converging habitat are also found in the edge region, in addition to those species that are most often found in the distinct environment of the edge.

Most backyards will not have enough room for long expanses of edge, but the effect can be created nonetheless. A cluster of trees surrounded by a ring of shrubs surrounded by a ring of flowers and grasses surrounded by open lawn will create several edge environments, albeit small ones. The "surrounded" in this example can be replaced with "bordered on three sides" or two sides. Trees planted at the edge of your property bordered by shrubs bordered by flowers and grasses and then bordered by open lawn is another approach.

TRADITIONAL VERSUS NATIVE GARDENS

MUCH OF WHAT YOU WILL read in this book could give the initial impression that bare lawn and domestic plants are worthless components of the backyard habitat. That is not the message that I want to impart to you.

Certainly, bare, tightly cropped lawn offers only limited food and shelter. But some species will be attracted to it. Mourning doves will find seed there, American robins will hunt for worms, swallows will swoop for flying insects, rabbits will munch on the grass and clover, mice and voles will roam the grassy jungle. Even a quick look down among the blades of grass will reveal a myriad of insect life.

Your vegetable and flower gardens play host to an even greater array of life. You already have more than a passing acquaintance with this fact if you've spent even one growing season in battle with the many invading pest species.

Developing a habitat for wildlife does not mean that you will need to do away with these elements. Incorporate them into your overall scheme.

The lawn actually serves several functions within the context of a backyard habitat. It provides open space between the various "wild" clusters, something that many species prefer to have in their living area. It maintains the traditional backyard appearance that may be important to neighbors and community standards. It allows avenues of sight for you to view wildlife in the other habitat elements. And, it maintains space for

whatever other uses you may have for the backyard – from play space for the children to a barbecue site.

You can enhance the wildlife value by adding tight-growing clovers to any future applications of grass seed. Among the various clovers that won't give the lawn a "weedy" appearance, white clover (*Trifolium repens*) is one of the most beneficial for wildlife. And, of course, the wildlife value of lawn or garden will skyrocket with the cessation of chemical use.

ABOVE: Earthworms are the measure of a healthy lawn. You will find large numbers of them in the soil of a lawn that hasn't been bombarded with a deadly array of chemicals. They are also primary food for many species of wildlife, such as birds and amphibians.

Many frustrations can be avoided from the start if you plan to separate your vegetable and flower gardens from the habitat portions of the backyard.

Native plants intended as habitat elements should not be planted with garden varieties or as borders around the gardens. Weeds should be controlled in and around the garden. A tightly mowed path of a couple feet around the garden areas should be maintained. A fence may be needed around the entire garden. Netting is a must over fruit-bearing crops; similar protection may be needed each spring to protect tender young plants from nipping beaks and incisors.

Traditional gardens, thus protected from many pest species, can also be enhanced in their offerings for wildlife not found as objectionable. Here, we are aiming primarily at butterflies and hummingbirds.

Many species of attractive wildflowers are discussed later in our chapter on butterflies (page 80), but domestic garden species also can be a magnet for these harmless, colorful insects. Some of the most effective are shown in the accompanying table.

For hummingbirds, just about any nectar-filled garden flower will do – so long as that flower is red. We'll discuss hummers in detail later in this book (page 92), but for now, let us just state that any garden within their range will stand a better chance of attracting the tiny birds if it offers an abundance of red flowers.

Garden Flowers Attractive to Butterflies

BOTANICAL NAME	COMMON NAME	BEST COLOR	HEIGHT (IN.)	REGIONS
Chrysanthemum spp.	chrysanthemums, daisies	red, purple	12–36	all
Cosmos spp.	cosmos	various	to 72	all
Dianthus barbatus	sweet William	red, red and white	12–24	all
Heliotropium arborescens	common heliotrope	purple	12–24	all
Iberis sempervirens	perennial candytuft	white	8–12	all
Impatiens wallerana	impatiens	red, orange	12–24	all
Lantana camara	lantana	red, yellow	12–36	all
Lavandula angustifolia	lavender	blue, violet	18	all
Nicotiana alata	flowering tobacco	red	24–36	all
Petunia x hybrida	petunia	red, pink, purple, yellow	12–18	all
Salvia splendens	scarlet sage	red	12–36	all
Sedum spectabile	showy stonecrop	red, pink	18–24	all
Tagetes erecta	African marigold	yellow, red	6–24	all
Tagetes patula	French marigold	gold with dark red	6–18	all
Zinnia elegans	zinnia	red, orange, yellow, pink	12–36	all

NATIVE VERSUS INTRODUCED PLANTS

In much of the following discussion, we will emphasize the use of native plants whenever possible. This is because those species growing wild in your area have passed through centuries adapting to your local weather and soil conditions. When you plant them in locations that provide the optimum amounts of sunlight, water, and nutrients (optimum for the particular plant species), they will adapt to the site and eventually provide nearly all of their own maintenance.

Native plants also will provide a more natural appearance to the habitat you are creating in the backyard. Many of our domesticated, introduced species, on the other hand, have been bred for the traditional garden mindset. They are intended to stand out from any natural plants they might be placed near. Their foreign, cultured appearance is intended to satisfy that traditional gardener's need to accomplish something. They look so different from what existed there previously and tell you that the gardener did the work.

This is one of the most difficult concepts for the new backyard habitatter to take to heart.

LEFT: The lowly dandelion is among the most hated of wild "invaders" on the traditional suburban lawn. But it is also a significant provider of food for a variety of wildlife species. This can be said of many plants branded as nuisances by traditional standards.

Sometimes, by doing less you've actually done more, from the perspective of attracting wildlife.

And, finally, I believe that the use of native plants in the backyard, in a small way, helps to repair at least some of the tremendous damage that has been done to the land. Let's face it, the house in which I sat to write this book and the house in which you are now sitting to read it both occupy land that once was covered with native plants and wildlife. It seems that backyard habitatting gives us the opportunity to return at least a little of the space to those that were here before.

However, I would not propose a totally purist attitude in this respect. Some of the native species listed in the following discussion are not always available through commercial suppliers. In those instances, a closely related domestic species is perfectly acceptable.

COLLECTING PLANTS AND SEEDS

It is possible to collect species from the wild, but only under very strict circumstances. The National Wildflower Research Center lists more than 2,500 species of native plants threatened with extinction. In our efforts to provide backyard habitat to wildlife, we must do nothing to further this dreadful situation. Certainly all of those threatened species must be left alone.

Limited seed collection in the wild, with permission of landowners, is acceptable. A passive, generally non-harmful method for this is

Native Grasses

The following native grasses are those that should thrive under most conditions within the region listed and yet not spread to uncontrollable "weed" status.

BOTANICAL NAME	COMMON NAME	HEIGHT (FT.)	HABITAT PREFERENCE
NORTHEAST			
Andropogon virginicus	broomsedge	3	fields, roadsides
Bouteloua curtipendula	sideoats grama grass	3	sandy soil
Chasmanthium latifolium	wild oats	3	waste places
Festuca elatior	tall fescue	3½	cultivated areas, roadsides
Koeleria cristata	June grass	1	dry, sandy soil
Panicum virgatum	switchgrass	4	moist, sandy soil
Schizachyrium scoparium	little bluestem	3	sandy soil
MIDWEST			
Andropogon gerardii	big bluestem	4½	sandy fields
Bouteloua curtipendula	sideoats grama grass	3	sandy soil
Panicum virgatum	switchgrass	4	moist, sandy soil
Sorghastrum avenaceum	Indian grass	6	dry fields
Stipa spartea	needlegrass	3	dry soil
SOUTHEAST			
Andropogon virginicus	broomsedge	3	fields, roadsides
Festuca ovina var. glauca	blue fescue	10in.	fields
Panicum virgatum	switchgrass	4	moist, sandy soil
Schizachyrium scoparium	little bluestem	3	sandy soil
SOUTHWEST			
Buchloe dactyloides	buffalo grass	8in.	dry soil
Oryzopsis hymenoides	Indian ricegrass	1½	fields
Panicum virgatum	switchgrass	4	moist, sandy soil
Schizachyrium scoparium	little bluestem	3	sandy soil
Sorghastrum avenaceum	Indian grass	6	dry fields
WEST			
Andropogon gerardii	big bluestem	4½	sandy fields
Bouteloua curtipendula	sideoats grama grass	3	sandy soil
Schizachyrium scoparium	little bluestem	3	sandy soil
Sorghastrum avenaceum	Indian grass	6	dry fields

to tie a fine-mesh material, cheese-cloth, or nylon stocking around the flowerhead of the desired plant just before it goes to seed. Shake the plant gently each day until a supply of seed has been deposited in your collecting material. As soon as a reasonable amount of seed has been obtained, remove the material. The plant probably will still have plenty of seed to spread into its natural environment.

Collection of entire wild plants from sites that are being cleared for development might even be applauded. If no other methods are under way to save any of the plants that would otherwise be bulldozed into oblivion, by all means seek permission to do the salvage work.

In most instances that follow, our references to native plants should be taken to mean buying these species from nurseries, garden centers, or other suppliers. Before buying, verify that the supplier is providing the plants from its own propagation efforts and not through collection from the wild.

NATIVE LAWNS

Somewhere between lawn and wildflower we find the native grasses, those hardy plants that seem to grab hold of any bit of soil available and then flourish. Many wildflower seed mixes will include seed for some of these plants as well because they are crucial to the success of any wildflower planting.

The wild grasses fill the niches between the wildflowers, giving a wildflower meadow or patch much of its field-like feel. They also do

much of the job of holding the soil in place against the effects of wind and rain.

These survivors have been known to catch the fancy of more than one backyard habitatter, becoming the central focus of his or her efforts. But, to lessen the potential for conflict with local "weed ordinances" and picky neighbors, a variety of wildflowers should be planted with the grasses. The grasses alone definitely can have a "weedy" appearance to the uninitiated eye.

Starting a stand of native grasses is at least a two-year process. Begin in late summer by repeatedly

ABOVE: Although we commonly use the term "grass" for any flat-bladed, short plant, there are actually more than 1,200 different native species of grass across North America. More than 150 other species have been introduced.

tilling the selected site of all vegetation. Be especially aggressive toward all introduced turf-type grasses, as these can compete successfully against the grasses you want to occupy that spot eventually. Continue the tilling throughout fall and then cover the area with a seed-free mulch or straw to prevent winter erosion.

Work the soil to a depth of about $\frac{1}{2}$ inch one more time, early in the next spring (before the last frost), and sow your seeds. An area of about 500 square feet should be sown with at least 2 ounces of grass seed. Roll the area to make sure that the seeds come into contact with the soil.

Freshly planted native grasses require water only if the spring rains are much less than normal or very sporadic. Even under these conditions, watering should be necessary only until germination has been achieved.

Contrary to what you might expect, the first-year plantings may not – probably will not – sprout and dominate the site like a new bed of lettuce. But, after another year or so, you should have a stand to rival anything in the wild.

The sanctuary provided by these tall grasses and the late summer/fall bounty of their seeds will attract an incredible array of insects and grassland birds, and these quickly colonize the new habitat. Small mammals will soon follow. Nests and burrows will appear, even if the warm-season grass habitat is limited to a small corner of the yard.

tiger salamander

KERRY (ABOVE), SUSAN, AND ELLEN GRIM OF HAMBURG, PENNSYLVANIA, HAVE SET OUT TO CREATE A BACKYARD HABITAT FOR WILDLIFE, BUT ALONG THE WAY THEY'VE ALSO DISCOVERED THE SIGNIFICANT LOW-MAINTENANCE QUALITY OF THEIR PLAN. THE NATIVE PLANTS THEY GROW IN PROFUSION ABOUT THE 17,000-SQUARE-FOOT PROPERTY LOOK AFTER THEMSELVES FOR THE MOST PART, JUST AS THEY WOULD IN THE WILDS OF THE APPALACHIAN REGION, AND, IN THEIR TURN, THEY SERVE THE NATIVE WILDLIFE QUITE WELL.

According to Kerry, a key to the impressive list of wildlife that the property attracts is diversity. The accompanying map of the habitat demonstrates this principle nicely. In the various plantings across the yard, the visitor finds a wide cross-section of native species rather than a large number of any single species. Such variety fulfills the needs of a much larger cross-section of the wildlife population.

Native plants like butterfly bush, TOP LEFT, and viburnum, LEFT, are well adapted to the soil and climate conditions in their regions, and are generally attractive to a wide range of wildlife species.

"Plan your plantings within defined areas rather than scatter them across the expanse of the property," he advises. "This makes maintenance much simpler."

For water, the Grims rely on a small recirculating pool. The "overgrown birdbath," as Kerry describes it, is 3 feet in diameter and 6 inches deep at most. The mini-pond's poured-concrete liner was installed in 1986.

Like any heavily used birdbath, the mini-pond needs its water changed regularly. But the Grims see this less as a chore than a necessary function to keep the wildlife coming. In addition to a wide variety of birds, the water source has attracted various amphibians. One green frog spent an entire summer in or near the mini-pond, becoming tame enough to accept offerings of Japanese beetles.

Only one or two neighbors maintain bird baths, and the nearest naturally constant water is about a half-mile away so according to Kerry, having some source of water is key to a successful habitat. He maintains the mini-pond's water level throughout the year, except during the coldest winter months.

He has also taken special pains to bring butterflies into this backyard by nurturing plantings of butterfly weed and butterfly bush. Spicebush swallowtails, black swallowtails, and mourning cloaks are some of the species that have rewarded these efforts, and monarchs have actually bred in this habitat.

Amid a planting of tea viburnum about 20 feet from the house,

a scattering of rocks – each one flat and about 1 or 2 feet in diameter – serves as feeding platforms for seed-eating birds. Kerry likes to feed them at ground level because of the diversity of birds that such a practice attracts.

However, a homemade feeder mounted on the rear deck had to be moved when a sharp-shinned hawk decided to make it his landing spot on his regular visits to the habitat. Fearing that the raptor would eventually collide with a window, Kerry relocated the feeder farther from the house. He never saw that sharp-shinned hawk take any of the backyard's collection of songbirds, but he has witnessed two such successful attacks: one by a broadwing hawk and one by an accipiter. Overall, however, he has had more problems with crows raiding the nests of other birds.

The Grims have lived on this property since 1982, when it supported only a few ornamental trees. They began to develop their habitat in 1983 and have seen the changes brought about by their efforts. For example, song sparrows now inhabit the area year-round and other birds have come to use the habitat for regular nesting activities. Grim's martin house attracts a small colony of purple martins, for which he stocks a platform feeder with ground eggshell. Among the other nesting species are mourning doves, American robins, chipping sparrows, cowbirds, house finches, house wrens, tree swallows, blue jays, and northern mockingbirds.

In addition, Kerry notes, "A lot

Many species find certain habitat elements particularly attractive. For example, nesting purple martins are drawn to the tray of crushed eggshell, while monarch butterflies feed on the clumps of milkweed, TOP LEFT, and bluebirds look for nestboxes in open areas near heavier cover, ABOVE. But a backyard filled with a variety of plant species, LEFT, often will attract a more diverse wildlife mix.

of birds that nest elsewhere in the neighborhood seem to end up in my yard after they've fledged. The cover and the water seem to attract them."

The Grim property lies about 250 feet from the edge of the

Some of the wildlife-attracting plants in the Grim habitat:

TREES
apple, birch, blue spruce, Canadian hemlock, chokecherry, Douglas fir, larch, mountain ash, mugo pine, Norway spruce, red oak, Sargent's crab apple, Scotch pine, Washington hawthorn, white pine

SHRUBS AND VINES
arborvitae, azalea, barberry, burning bush, butterfly bush, Carolina shrub, honeysuckle, juniper, lilac, monarda, Oregon grape holly, rhododendron, sedum, tea viburnum, trumpet vine, yucca

FLOWERS AND HERBS
abelia, butterfly weed, common milkweed, wildflower (various species), and wild grass (various species)

Some of the wildlife sighted in the Grim habitat:

BIRDS
accipiter hawk, American robin, black-capped chickadee, blue jay, broadwing hawk, cedar waxwing, chipping sparrow, common crow, cowbird, dickcissel, house finch, house sparrow, house wren, junco, mourning dove, northern cardinal, northern mockingbird, purple martin, sapsucker, sharp-shinned hawk, song sparrow, tree swallow, white-throated sparrow

MAMMALS
chipmunk, cottontail rabbit, gray squirrel, meadow vole, red squirrel, short-tailed shrew, striped skunk

REPTILES AND AMPHIBIANS
Green frog, salamander (various species)

INSECTS AND ARACHNIDS
black swallowtails, crickets (various species), monarchs, mourning cloaks, praying mantises, spicebush swallowtails

Many fruit-bearing plants, like the crab apple, ABOVE, will hold their fruit through much of the winter, providing a ready supply of food for many songbird species that generally do not come to feeders. Most plants, however, like the sedum, BELOW, provide their crops only during the warmer seasons.

forest, and gray and red squirrels occasionally turn up at their bird feeders. But most of the squirrels don't bother to travel the extra distance across neighbors' properties, as they can feed heavily in the wooded area.

The Grim's "wild" property and the wildlife it attracts have not caused problems with the neighbors. "As long as you cut your weeds around here everything is fine," Kerry notes. That can be a tall assignment for him, as one of his "weeds" is crown vetch, planted across much of the property by the previous owners. It can grow so fast that he can't keep up with it at times.

Future plans include the planting of additional viburnums, both for their low-maintenance qualities and for the wildlife-nurturing berry crops that they produce each year. In addition, Kerry wants to hang more hollowed gourds by the martin house like those he offered the purple martins with such success.

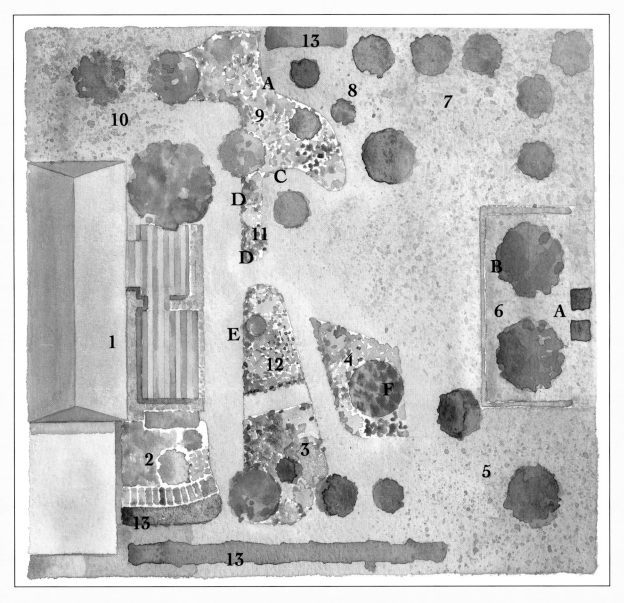

GRIM HABITAT

1 house with deck out front and driveway to right

2 steps leading from driveway; 30-inch tall juniper groundcover beneath birch and mugo pine; shrubs

3 Douglas fir, mountain ash, red chokeberry, Sargent's crab apple, mugo pine, shrubs

4 juniper, lilac, sedum, yucca

5 Sargent's crab apple, white pine

6 stone wall enclosing red oaks with understory of very small rhododendron; garden plots in back

7 Canadian hemlocks

8 mixed trees

9 birch, larch, mixed shrubs

10 Scotch pine, white pine

11 lilac, viburnum

12 mixed shrubs

13 arborvitae

A house wren nest box

B elevated tray full of eggshells for purple martin, house finch and mourning dove

C covered bird feeder

D rocks used for feeding platforms

E mini-pool

F purple martin nest box

THE WILDFLOWER GARDEN

MOST MUNICIPALITIES HAVE "weed ordinances" that in their uninformed passage declare most true habitats as unwanted within their boundaries. These came from a mindset that believed carefully manicured lawns in neat one-after-the-other rows were what a town really should look like. In the minds' eyes of the governing officials that fostered these ordinances, the ideal community would look much like those fictional television burgs through which Beaver Cleaver and Dennis the Menace rode their bicycles.

These ordinances prove very useful to those neighbors who still subscribe to that 1950s vision of community and who wish not to be "bothered" with any plants, or wildlife, that aren't neat and tidy in the conventional wisdom.

Your best defense against this attitude is to talk over your plans with your neighbors, explaining what you are doing and especially why some of your backyard may soon appear unmowed or "wild" in other ways.

Once you feel comfortable that a plot of wildflowers and grasses will be acceptable in your neighborhood, there are many commercially available seed mixes that you can find at the local garden center. Many of today's mixes are adjusted nicely for certain regions, avoiding some of the problems that the original non-specific mixes entailed.

However, your healthiest, most vibrant species are the native plants waiting nearby for the opportunity to colonize any space you're willing

Wildflowers for Seasonal Color

This table should help you to select native wildflowers that will provide color throughout the growing season in your region.

* A – Annual, B – Biennial, P – Perennial
**NE – Northeast, SE – Southeast, MW – Midwest, SW – Southwest, NW – Northwest, W – West

BOTANICAL NAME	COMMON NAME	FLOWER COLOR	HEIGHT (IN.)	LIFE CYCLE*	REGIONS**
SPRING					
Anemone patens	pasque flower	lavender, blue, white	6	P	W
Aquilegia caerulea	blue columbine	blue	24	P	SW W
Aquilegia canadensis	wild columbine	red and yellow	36	P	NE SE MW SW
Aquilegia chrysantha	golden columbine	yellow	24–48	P	W
Aquilegia formosa	sitka columbine	red	24	P	W
Baptisia australis	blue false indigo	blue	36–48	P	NE SE W
Camassia quamash	common camas	blue-violet	12–18	P	NW W
Castilleja indivisa	Texas paintbrush	red	16	A/B	SW
Claytonia lanceolata	spring beauty	white, pink	4–8	P	W
Claytonia virginica	spring beauty	pink	4–6	P	NE SE MW NW
Collinsia heterophylla	Chinese-houses	white and lavender	24	A	SW NW
Delphinium cardinale	scarlet larkspur	red	48	P	NE W
Dodecatheon meadia	shooting-star	pink	10–15	P	MW
Erythronium americanum	fawn lily	yellow	4–10	P	NE SE NW W
Eschscholzia californica	California poppy	orange	18	A/P	SW NW W
Fritillaria lanceolata	mission bells	yellow	12–48	P	W
Fritillaria pudica	yellow bell	yellow	4–12	P	SW W
Geranium maculatum	wild geranium	magenta	12–24	P	NE SE MW
Iris cristata	crested iris	blue, purple	4–9	P	NE SE MW SW
Iris missouriensis	western blue flag	pale blue	20	P	SW NW W
Iris tenax	tough leaf iris	lavender	16	P	NW W
Layia platyglossa	tidy-tips	yellow and white	12	A	SW
Linanthus grandiflorus	mountain phlox	white, pink, lavender	14	A	SW NW
Linum perenne subsp. lewisii	prairie flax	blue	24	P	SE NW W
Lupinus perennis	wild lupine	blue, purple	12–24	P	MW NW

BOTANICAL NAME	COMMON NAME	COLOR	HEIGHT	CYCLE*	REGIONS**
Lupinus subcarnosus	bluebonnet	blue	12–24	A	SW
Lupinus texensis	Texas bluebonnet	blue	12–24	A	SW
Mentzelia lindleyi	blazing star	yellow	12–48	A	SW
Nemophila menziesii	baby-blue-eyes	blue	10	A	SW
Penstemon digitalis	foxglove penstemon	white	48	P	NE SE MW SW W
Penstemon smallii	beardtongue	purple	36	P	SE
Phacelia campanularia	desert bell	blue	8–30	A	SW
Phlox divaricata	wild blue phlox	blue	8–12	A	NE SE MW
Phlox drummondii	annual phlox	red	10–20	A	SW
Sisyrinchium angustifolium	blue-eyed grass	blue	6–10	P	NE SE MW SW NW W
Stokesia laevis	Stokes' aster	purple, blue	24	P	SE
Stylomecon heterophylla	wind poppy	red-orange	24	A	SW
Viola cornuta	horned violet	yellow and purple	5–8	P	MW
SUMMER					
Asclepias incarnata	swamp milkweed	pink	48	P	NE SE MW SW
Asclepias tuberosa	butterfly milkweed	orange	12–36	P	NE SE MW SW NW W
Baptisia australis	blue false indigo	blue	36–48	P	NE SE MW SW
Bidens aristosa	tickseed sunflower	yellow	12–60	A	NE
Campanula rotundifolia	bluebell	blue	6–20	P	NE SE SW W
Castilleja coccinea	Indian-paintbrush	red	12–24	A/B	NE SE
Clarkia amoena	farewell-to-spring	lavender, pink, white	12–36	A	SW NW
Clarkia concinna	red-ribbons	pink	18	A	SW NW
Clarkia pulchella	deerhorn clarkia	pink, magenta	8–18	A	SW W
Clarkia unguiculata	elegant clarkia	salmon, purple	36	A	SW NW
Collinsia heterophylla	Chinese-houses	white and lavender	24	A	SW NW
Coreopsis lanceolata	lance-leaved coreopsis	yellow	24	P	NE SE SW
Coreopsis tinctoria	annual coreopsis	red, yellow	8	A	SW
Delphinium cardinale	scarlet larkspur	red	48	P	NW
Delphinium virescens	prairie larkspur	white	60	P	SW

(continued)

to give them. This is generally true, unless you live in the center of a large development, where all native vegetation has been removed. And, even here, the native plants will probably be reclaiming some of their former range.

Plan your wildflower/wild grass site in a half-dozen or so strips of generally uniform width. Till one strip each year in sequence. After you have tilled the final strip, begin the same sequence once again. This method will favor the faster-growing flowers and grasses over shrubs and trees.

Wildlife and winds will supply plenty of seed for these strips. But, if there is a wild area near your home that holds an especially appealing mix of wild plants and you can get the owner's permission, feel free to help the natural processes along. In late summer and early fall, when the plants are releasing their seeds, spread an old sheet downwind on a dry sunny day. When a supply of seed has collected, fold the sheet in on itself, carry it to your strip, and shake.

COLOR FOR THE NEIGHBORS

In selecting wildflower species, you might want to choose a range that will produce their blooms in sequence from early spring through fall. This constant barrage of color will go a long way toward convincing neighbors that the site is indeed a flower bed and not some untended menagerie of invading weeds, poised for an attack on their property.

BOTANICAL NAME	COMMON NAME	COLOR	HEIGHT	CYCLE*	REGIONS**
Dodecatheon meadia	shooting-star	pink	10–15	P	NE SE
Dodecatheon pulchellum	western shooting-star	pink	10–15	P	SW
Dracopis amplexicaulis	coneflower	yellow	24–36	A	MW
Echinacea purpurea	purple coneflower	purple	24–36	P	NE SE MW
Epilobium angustifolium	fireweed	pink-red	24–72	P	NE SE SW NW W
Erigeron speciosus	Oregon fleabane	white, blue	24	P	SW NW W
Eriogonum umbellatum	sulphur flower	orange, yellow	4–12	P	SW NW W
Eschscholzia californica	California poppy	orange	18	A/P	SW NW W
Eupatorium maculatum	Joe-pye weed	pink-purple	72	P	SE
Gaillardia spp.	blanket flowers	red and yellow	18–24	P	SE SW W
Geranium viscosissimum	red wild geranium	purple-pink	24	P	W
Geum triflorum	prairie smoke	purple	12–18	P	W
Helenium autumnale	sneezeweed	yellow-orange	24–48	P	NE SE MW SW NW W
Helianthus angustifolius	swamp sunflower	yellow	72	A	NE
Helianthus annuus	common sunflower	yellow	36–96	A	NE SE SW NW W
Ipomopsis rubra	standing cypress	red	24–72	P/B	SE SW
Liatris punctata	dotted gayfeather	violet	24	P	W
Liatris pycnostachya	Kansas gayfeather	violet, lavender	24–48	P	SE SW
Liatris scariosa	tall gayfeather	violet, lavender	10–20	P	NE
Liatris spicata	spike gayfeather	violet	24–36	P	NE
Lilium canadense	Canada lily	orange	108	P	NE SE
Linanthus grandiflorus	mountain phlox	white, pink, lavender	14	A	SW NW
Lupinus perennis	wild lupine	blue, purple	12–24	P	NE SE
Lupinus succulentus	succulent lupine	purple	24–48	A	SW
Machaeranthera tanacetifolia	Tahoka daisy	lavender with yellow centers	18	A/B	SW W
Mirabilis multiflora	wild four o'clock	red, pink, yellow, white	48	P	SW

PLANT LIFESPAN

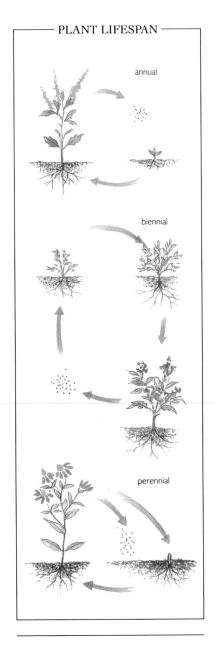

annual

biennial

perennial

ABOVE: Herbaceous plants, like grasses and wildflowers, are of three types: annual, which live their entire lives in one year; biennial, which live two years, produce seeds, and die; and perennial, which live several years.

BOTANICAL NAME	COMMON NAME	COLOR	HEIGHT	CYCLE*	REGIONS**
Monarda citriodora	lemon mint	pink or white with purple spots	24	A	SW
Monarda didyma	bee balm	red	48	P	NE SE
Monarda fistulosa	bergamot	pink, lavender	24–36	P	NE SE SW
Oenothera biennis	evening primrose	yellow	24–48	B	NE SE MW SW
Oenothera caespitosa	gumbo lily	yellow	24–48	B	NW
Oenothera missouriensis	Ozark sundrops	yellow	16–20	B	SW
Oenothera speciosa	showy evening primrose	pink	24–36	B	SE
Penstemon barbatus	common beard-tongue	red	24–48	P	W
Petalostemon purpureum	prairie clover	purple-red	12–36	P	MW
Phlox drummondii	annual phlox	red	10–20	A	SE SW
Ratibida columnaris	prairie coneflower	yellow, yellow and red	36	P	SW W
Rudbeckia hirta	black-eyed Susan	yellow	24–36	P	NE SE SW
Rudbeckia laciniata	coneflower	yellow	36–96	P	SE
Salvia coccinea	Texas sage	red	24	P	SE SW
Solidago odora	sweet goldenrod	yellow	36	P	NE SE SW
Tradescantia virginiana	common spiderwort	purple, white	12–24	P	SE SW
Verbena stricta	hoary vervain	purple	24–36	P	MW W
Vernonia altissima	ironweed	purple	60	P	NE SE
FALL Asclepias incarnata	swamp milkweed	pink	48	P	NE SE MW SW
Aster azureus	blue aster	blue	48	P	NE
Aster cordifolius	blue wood aster	blue-violet	72	P	NE
Aster ericoides	heath aster	white	36–60	P	SW
Aster laevis	smooth aster	pale blue, purple	42	P	SE
Aster lateriflorus	calico aster	purple, white	48	P	SE
Aster lineariifolius	aster	violet	24	P	SE SW
Aster novae-angliae	New England aster	pink, lavender	36–60	P	NE SE MW
Bidens aristosa	tickseed sunflower	yellow	12–60	A	NE SE MW SW
Echinacea purpurea	purple coneflower	purple	24–36	P	NE SE
Eriogonum umbellatum	sulphur flower	orange, yellow	4–12	P	W

(continued)

ABOVE: Flat-topped rocks make an attractive backdrop for mixed plantings of wildflowers and help to anchor the landscape.

BOTANICAL NAME	COMMON NAME	COLOR	HEIGHT	CYCLE*	REGIONS**
Eupatorium maculatum	Joe-pye weed	pink-purple	72	P	MW
Helianthus angustifolius	swamp sunflower	yellow	72	A	MW
Helianthus annuus	common sunflower	yellow	36–96	A	NE SE SW NW W
Helianthus maximilianii	Maximilian sunflower	yellow	72	A	SW
Liatris punctata	dotted gayfeather	violet	24	P	SW
Machaeranthera tanacetifolia	prairie aster	lavender with yellow centers	18	A/B	SW W
Oenothera biennis	evening primrose	yellow	24–48	B	NE SE SW
Solidago altissima	tall goldenrod	yellow	36–72	P	SW
Solidago californica	California goldenrod	yellow	24–48	P	NW
Solidago canadensis	Canada goldenrod	yellow	24–48	P	W
Solidago nemoralis	gray goldenrod	yellow	24	P	NE SE
Solidago odora	sweet goldenrod	yellow	36	P	NE SE
Solidago sempervirens	seaside goldenrod	yellow	72	P	NE SE
Solidago spp.	goldenrods	yellow	24–72	P	MW
Vernonia altissima	ironweed	purple	60	P	SE MW
Vernonia noveboracensis	New York ironweed	purple	36–72	P	NE SE

BELOW: A flock of American goldfinches feeds on the seeds in a patch of thistle. The plant can be a noxious weed, spreading rapidly and controlled only by great effort, but it is also a favorite food source for many desirable bird species.

STEM CUTTINGS

RIGHT: Cut 6 to 12 inches from the end of a stem. Remove stem tip. Keeping six leaves, make a diagonal cut about 4 to 8 inches down and discard the remainder. Remove lower two leaves, leaving their axillary buds. Dip stem in rooting hormone and insert in moist rooting medium, covering the nodes of the two leaves you removed. Keep humid and in bright shade until the new roots are at least 1 inch long.

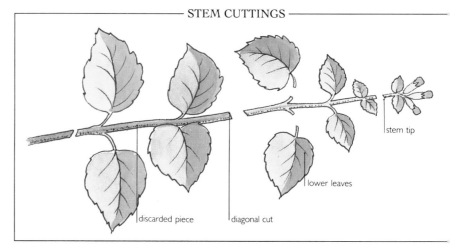

discarded piece

diagonal cut

lower leaves

stem tip

A NEW PERSPECTIVE ON WEEDS

A WEED IN THE BROADEST definition is any plant growing where a human doesn't want it to grow. In the traditional use of the word it has most often been applied to wild, native plants.

But in our new view as habitatters, intent on establishing communities of native plants and wildlife in our backyards, a weed can be a non-native ornamental, a wild plant native to another region of the continent, or an invasive native species. Any plant that doesn't work to meet the needs of wildlife and to fulfill our goal of attracting wildlife into the backyard is a weed to us, at least within that area of the backyard that we have determined will be our wildlife habitat.

Given this new perspective, a plant really has to work at it to be seen as a weed. Since most native plants provide some benefit to wildlife, the real definition of a weed in a natural garden involves: a particularly invasive nature, to the extent that other plants are out-competed for available space; an unappealing appearance; or being out of context with the rest of the site.

Even some of the highly invasive weed species listed in the table on page 32 have significant wildlife value. For example, considering only some of the most common butterflies, we find:

• Black-eyed Susan (*Rudbeckia hirta*) is a nectar source for the great spangled fritillary and pearly crescentspot.

• Plantains and chicory (*Plantago* spp. and *Cichorium intybus*) are caterpillar food plants and nectar sources for the buckeye.

• Thistles (*Cirsium* spp.) are caterpillar food plants for the painted lady and nectar sources for the pipevine swallowtail, tiger swallowtail, western tiger swallowtail, spicebush swallowtail, dogface butterfly, gulf fritillary, pearly crescentspot, Milbert's tortoiseshell, American painted lady, red admiral, viceroy, monarch, silverspotted skipper, fiery skipper, and tawny-edged skipper.

• Milkweeds (*Asclepias* spp.) are essential caterpillar food plants for the monarch and queen, but also provide nectar for the pipevine swallowtail, eastern black swallowtail, giant swallowtail, tiger swallowtail, western tiger swallowtail, spicebush swallowtail, checkered white, cabbage white, common sulphur, orange sulphur, gray hairstreak, spring azure, common blue, great spangled fritillary, pearly crescentspot, question mark, mourning cloak, American painted lady, painted lady, red admiral, viceroy, monarch, queen, hackberry butterfly, and fiery skipper.

• Daisies (*Chrysanthemum* spp.) are nectar sources for the cloudless giant sulphur, pearly crescentspot, Milbert's tortoiseshell, red admiral, queen, and fiery skipper.

• Queen-Anne's-lace (*Daucus carota* subsp. *carota*) provides food for the caterpillar of the eastern black swallowtail and nectar for the adults of the eastern black swallowtail and gray hairstreak.

• Sweet pea (*Lathyrus odoratus*) is both a caterpillar food plant and nectar source for the gray hairstreak, and a nectar source for the marine blue and silvery blue.

As you can see, the definition of a weed is now much more subjective and personal than ever before. It's also much more regional because varying growing conditions from area to area will render the same plant species invasive in one spot and totally controllable – even desirable – in another.

THINK BEFORE YOU WEED

Physical removal is the desired method for dealing with weeds. Mow them down, dig them out.

Herbicides are not something that we encourage. They are much too destructive to the overall environment. Many are not very specific to the plants they affect. And some are incredibly long-lasting once applied. They could actually thwart your future efforts.

Many of the most desirable wildflowers and other wild plants are highly susceptible to the effects of herbicides, in even small amounts. In addition, the use of these chemicals will quickly remove the pollinating insects, such as bees and butterflies, that these plants need for seed and fruit production from the local environment.

Before any measures at all are taken against a weed (following our new definition of the word), make absolutely certain that there is no purpose for it to serve in the habitat. Often young plants will take years to reach the stage of the mature plant that you are planning to remove. The existing plant, if healthy and thriving, has proven its ability to survive in this exact location. Are you sure that it is of no use to wildlife?

Also, be aware – in detail – of everything that grows at all times of the year in the spot from which you are planning to remove that one plant. Perhaps another season will reveal something that is quite desirable and possibly difficult to obtain or establish, something that you definitely don't want to lose. You might need to consider a gentler, less destructive means for removing the undesirable plant to avoid removal of the other species as well.

The Worst Invaders

The following species are the worst offenders as invaders of growing space and successful competitors against other plants within the regions listed. They include both natives and aliens to the regions listed. In other regions they are not as invasive and may even be a recommended species. Some of them are contained in some commercially available seed mixes.

*NE – Northeast, SE – Southeast, MW – Midwest, SW – Southwest, NW – Northwest, W – West

BOTANICAL NAME	COMMON NAME	REGIONS*
Achillea millefolium	common yarrow	SE MW SW W
Agropyron repens	quackgrass	all
Anagallis arvensis	pimpernel	SW
Asclepias syriaca	common milkweed	MW
Bidens aristosa	tickseed sunflower	SE SW
Bidens polylepis	tickseed sunflower	SE
Campanula rapunculoides	creeping bellflower	MW
Capsella bursa-pastoris	shepherd's purse	all
Centaurea cyanus	bachelor's button	NE SE MW NW SW
Centaurea spp.	knapweeds	W
Cerastium vulgatum	mouse-eared chickweed	all
Chrysanthemum carinatum	painted daisy	NW
Chrysanthemum coronarium	garland chrysanthemum	SW NW
Chrysanthemum leucanthemum	oxeye daisy	NE MW NW SW W
Cichorium intybus	chicory	SE MW SW NW
Cirsium arvense	Canadian thistle	all
Cynodon dactylon	Bermuda grass	all
Daucus carota subsp. carota	Queen-Anne's-lace	all
Digitaria sanguinalis	hairy crabgrass	all
Eleusine indica	goose grass	all
Erigeron spp.	fleabanes	SW
Eschscholzia californica	California poppy	SW
Eupatorium maculatum	Joe-pye weed	NE
Glechoma hederacea	ground ivy	all
Gypsophila paniculata	baby's breath	W
Helianthus annuus	common sunflower	MW SW
Helianthus grosseserratus	sunflower	MW
Helianthus mollis	downy sunflower	MW
Lathyrus latifolius	perennial sweet pea	MW NW W
Linaria genistifolia subsp. dalmatica	dalmatian toadflax	W
Linaria maroccana	spurred snapdragon	NW
Linaria vulgaris	butter and eggs	SE MW NW W
Lobularia maritima	sweet alyssum	NW SW
Lythrum salicaria	purple loosestrife	NE
Mirabilis jalapa	four o'clock	SE MW
Plantago major	broadleaf plantain	all

BOTANICAL NAME	COMMON NAME	REGIONS*
Poa annua	annual bluegrass	all
Polygonum persicaria	lady's thumb	all
Prunella vulgaris	heal-all	SE NW
Pueraria lobata	kudzu	all
Rhus radicans	poison ivy	all
Rudbeckia hirta	black-eyed Susan	NW W
Salvia lyrata	lyre-leafed sage	SE
Saponaria officinalis	soapwort	SE SW
Setaria glauca	yellow foxtail	all
Sorghum halepense	Johnson grass	all
Tradescantia virginiana	spiderwort	NE
Verbascum thapsus	mullein	NE SE NW SW W

OPPOSITE: The oxeye daisy, shown here with another invasive wildflower, hawkweed (yellow flowers), is one of the most pervasive of wild plants.

BELOW: Although many wild plant species are commonly regarded as "weeds" in the backyard, to the wildlife gardener they can be some of the most attractive plants available. They are cheap, flower beautifully, and have incredible drawing power for many butterfly, other insect, and bird species.

THE SPECIAL APPEAL OF HEDGEROWS AND THICKETS

BOTH HEDGEROWS AND fencerows are a lost treasure across much of the continent today. They are missed, both by wildlife and wildlife enthusiasts, for they have long been prime components of a habitat. In even a short length of one of these rows, wildlife can find all the basic needs of life in addition to secret and protected travel routes.

In form they are simple affairs: lengths of shrubs, stunted trees, vines, and small herbaceous plants intergrown tightly a few feet wide, along the edge of a field or yard. The thornier and more clinging the plants, the better for wildlife. Wildlife trails of varying sizes and durations wind their way through the stems.

The hedges that many owners now line their properties with are reminiscent of those magnificent tangles. But they are generally composed of one species of plant, kept tightly cropped on all sides. They provide some cover and food, but very little in comparison to their wild ancestors.

Hedgerows and fencerows were commonly found throughout agricultural regions from the time that the first generations of farmers began to plow sections of the continent. But, as clearcut farming and potent herbicides came into use, the edges of fields became parts of much bigger fields and the tangles were gone.

You can regain this portion of our heritage in your backyard

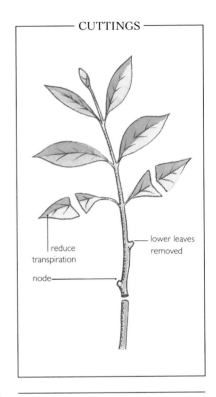

CUTTINGS

reduce transpiration

node

lower leaves removed

ABOVE: Many plants can be collected in the wild, with permission, from branch and twig cuttings and planted directly into the backyard habitat. Removing the lowest sets of leaves and planting a bit deeper than those leaves will give the cutting an extra boost, as will rooting hormone at the base cut.

LEFT: Your neighbors may be most comfortable with your efforts for wildlife, particularly the "weeds" you may want to add to your property, if you are careful to plant them ornamentally. Small groupings, located at corners, around fence posts or trees, and the like, may best fit in with the conventions of your neighborhood. Most wildlife species will be able to take advantage of the plants in this arrangement, provided the plantings are not too small.

habitat. Begin with the thorniest, most heavily fruiting shrub species you can find. Many commercially available species will serve wildlife's needs quite nicely. The table on page 43 shows some of the most promising native species.

Plant these shrubs much tighter than suggested by the commercial suppliers. Leave only about half the recommended space between plants. Break up the uniformity of this line of shrubs with an evergreen tree or two and add several strong, fruit-bearing vines at regular intervals. Into this you can toss wildflower and "weed" seeds at random or allow the birds to carry their favorite seeds there (as explained on page 36).

Your entire hedgerow may be only a dozen feet or so in length and only 2 or 3 feet wide, but you will be amazed at the variety of wildlife you will see there. Of course, the larger the hedgerow, the more benefit to wildlife.

The plow-perch method is a natural way to let the birds develop a hedgerow or thicket for you. In

LEFT: This barberry *(Berberis)* hedgerow is about 150 feet in length and 6 feet wide at some spots and runs along the side of my father's property in central Pennsylvania. It provides shelter for cottontail rabbits and various small rodents, nesting cover for as many as a half-dozen pairs of birds in some years, and a year-round supply of berries that has kept resident mockingbirds in place for more than three decades.

summer or early fall, till the area where you want the new growth, in the shape that you want the hedgerow or thicket to be when it matures.

Set posts at 15-foot intervals across this area, again in the eventual shape you're trying for, and string strong twine or wire between these posts. A double row in a straight line will produce a dense hedgerow, while a double or triple row in concentric circles will generate a protective maze of thicket.

Fruit- and seed-eating birds will perch on your posts and wires. And, as you already know, where a bird perches a bird leaves the remains of a recent meal. In this way the birds will plant their preferred food species, both wild and domestic, exactly where you want your new hedgerow or thicket. Barberry (Berberis spp.), black-

LEFT: One of more than 30 mockingbird nests that have been built over the years in the barberry (Berberis) hedge shown on page 35. The survival rate of the young birds fledged during that period has averaged less than one per year because of free-roaming house cats.

RIGHT: Two unconventional but productive methods of propagating new woody plants from existing ones are air layering (left) and underground layering. In the first, a strip of bark is removed and the wound is wrapped in sphagnum moss and plastic wrap. In the latter, the leaves are trimmed from much of the stem, which is then buried under the soil and held in place with a stake.

METHODS OF PROPAGATION

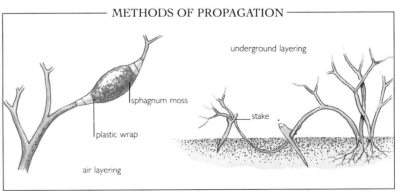

underground layering

sphagnum moss

plastic wrap

stake

air layering

berry (Rubus spp.), blueberry (Vaccinium spp.), crabapple (Malus spp.), dogwood (Cornus spp.), elderberry (Sambucus spp.), holly (Ilex spp.), honeysuckle (Lonicera spp.), mulberry (Morus spp.), raspberry (Rubus spp.), serviceberry (Amelanchier spp.), sumac (Rhus spp.), and wild cherry (Prunus spp.) are just some of the species that the birds will contribute.

Such sites generally take hold and grow into mature hedgerows or thickets as quickly as those planted with root stock. This is the method that Nature has employed for centuries along fencerows, which are generally accepted as one key to many successful wildlife populations.

BELOW: The coyote, common resident of the North American West for thousands of years, has steadily expanded its range to the north and east during the past few decades. This is due to the disappearance of larger predators, such as wolves.

SOUTHEAST GARDEN

MURREL CREEKMORE (ABOVE) HAS
LIVED ON HIS 42,000-SQUARE-FOOT
TWIN BRANCH DRIVE PROPERTY IN
MARIETTA, GEORGIA, SINCE 1969.
IT IS A WILDLIFE OASIS AMID A
BURGEONING SPRAWL OF SUBURBAN
DEVELOPMENT. "THERE'S JUST NO
ROOM LEFT FOR ANYTHING —
WILDLIFE, THAT IS," HE SAYS,
POINTING OUT THAT THE LAST
14 UNDEVELOPED ACRES IN HIS
NEIGHBORHOOD RECENTLY FELL
VICTIM TO THE BULLDOZER.

Murrel Creekmore advocates doing as
much as you can, whenever and
wherever you can, for wildlife. His
backyard attests to that conviction.
Many different types of habitat have
been provided, including this glade-
like setting with its stone wall
centerpiece, TOP. He also feeds heavily,
offering many types of seed in
different feeding situations, ABOVE.

Exactly the opposite process
has been taking place on the
Creekmore property. Most of the
considerable number of oak and
hickory trees have been added by
Creekmore. He has also planted
some pear trees, the fruit of which
is harvested mostly by the neighborhood's sizeable squirrel population. Similarly, the birds take two-
thirds and more of Creekmore's
three 50-foot-long beds of strawberries (he only covers one of the
three beds with protective netting),

and nearly all the blackberries
and grapes. "I'm kind of tender-
hearted," he explains. "I like to be
kind to animals." And, in general,
the birds provide more benefit than
harm through the insects they eat.

In addition to the food plants,
which also include various conifers,
Creekmore follows a philosophy
that he offers as key advice to any
beginner wildlife gardener: "Save
any kind of food plant. It doesn't
matter if it's only a pokeberry.
That's still enough to feed a bird
for a day or two." He puts similar
emphasis on plants that provide
cover, including extensive hedgerows of privet, dogwood, and
honeysuckle, and thick clusters of
ivy and azalea.

A heavy growth of privet covers
his brush pile and its wildlife value
has been extended by persuading
his backyard neighbor to locate
another brush pile close by. The
resulting dense cover has, among
other things, provided a sheltered
spot for a mother opossum to raise
her young.

In open areas where nothing
special has been planted for
wildlife, Creekmore has mulched
heavily. This has sliced his mowing

gray squirrel

time from almost four hours (when the property had "as much grass as possible") to practically nothing. But, more important, the "millions of worms" that such an environment supports provide an abundant food source for many birds.

Water poses no problem in Creekmore's habitat, which includes two small spring-fed streams. Although these flow year-round and support populations of native minnows, neither stream is much deeper than 2 feet or wider than 8 feet. Creekmore has placed two poured-concrete footbridges across the water, one of which has railings covered with jasmine. He

has also created a privet hedgerow along a section of one stream, and the extra shelter and warmth this gives has proved very attractive to birds in winter.

But, as with most aspects of his backyard haven, Creekmore has not been content to rely solely on what nature has provided. Four years ago he created a PVC-lined pond – 8 feet by 12 feet by about 2 feet deep. This mini-pond was stocked with a half-dozen domestic goldfish. Four were lost almost immediately to predators, but the remaining two have reproduced and now the total population has risen to 50 or 60.

ABOVE: Black-eyed Susan can be an aggressive invader, but it also provides food for birds, butterflies, moths, and other insects.

Nature also has provided inhabitants for the pond, including at least four bullfrogs, innumerable snails, boatmen, dragonfly larvae, and many other insect species. Raccoon and bird tracks attest to the attraction that the water holds for nearly all wildlife. The pond freezes over, but Creekmore melts holes with pans of hot water.

Although his neighbors haven't followed Creekmore's example

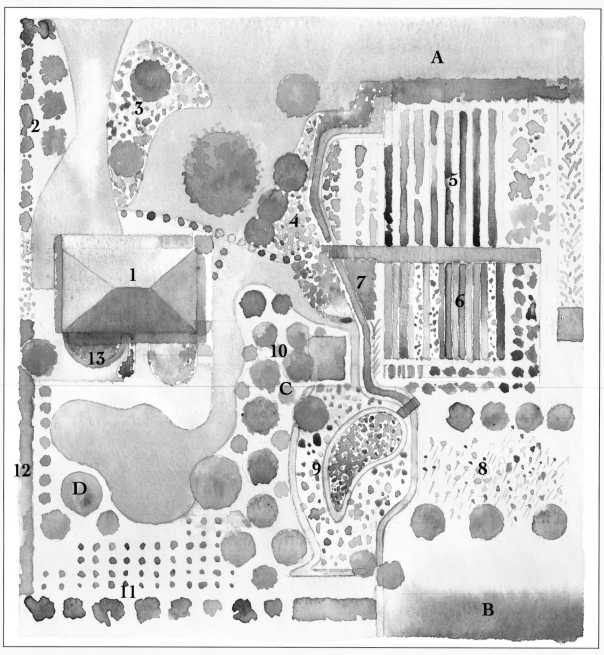

CREEKMORE HABITAT
1 house and driveway
2 honeysuckle and dogwood edging;
hickory, oak, and white pine
3 bulbs beneath mixed trees
4 flowers, mixed trees
5 raised vegetable beds

6 seedlings, wildflowers, onions,
strawberries, blueberries; shed
7 herbs
8 grass, wildflowers, mixed trees
9 shade garden, flower beds
10 mixed trees; barn-style building
11 mixed trees, dogwood edging

12 privet
13 azaleas, ivy; rock wall

A heavily mulched, raised bed
B brush pile, privet, and bamboo
C owl box
D fish pond

Some of the wildlife-attracting plants found in the Creekmore habitat:

TREES
Bradford pear, cherry, fig, gum, hickory, magnolia, oak, pear, poplar, redbud, Virginia pine, white pine

SHRUBS AND VINES
bamboo, blackberry, blueberry, dogwood, domestic grape, elderberry, honeysuckle, ivy, laurel, privet

FLOWERS AND HERBS
azalea, bee balm, impatiens, phlox, sedum, strawberry, sweet William, wildflower (various species), and wild grass (various species)

Some of the wildlife sighted in the Creekmore habitat:

BIRDS
American goldfinch, American robin, black-capped chickadee, blue jay, bobwhite quail, brown thrasher, common crow, common grackle, Cooper's hawk, cowbird, downy woodpecker, eastern bluebird, European starling, evening grosbeak, house wren, indigo bunting, mourning dove, nothern cardinal, northern flicker, northern mockingbird, pileated woodpecker, pine siskin, purple finch, red-bellied woodpecker, red-headed woodpecker, red-winged blackbird, rufous hummingbird, rufous-sided towhee, screech owl, sparrow (various species), tufted titmouse, Virginia rail, white-breasted nuthatch, yellow-bellied woodpecker

MAMMALS
chipmunk, cottontail rabbit, flying squirrel, gray squirrel, mouse, muskrat, opossum, raccoon, rat

REPTILES AND AMPHIBIANS
black snake, bullfrog, box turtle, copperhead snake, frog and treefrog (various species), garter snake, ringneck snake, salamander (various species), snapping turtle, toad (various species), water snake

INSECTS AND ARACHNIDS
boatmen, butterflies, caddis flies, damsel-flies, dragonflies, leafhoppers, spiders.

OTHERS
crayfish, minnows, snails

to any great degree, neither have they shown any concern over the "wild" area next door. The only problem has arisen with some neighborhood cats that occasionally take a songbird or two.

Creekmore hasn't sacrificed any normal backyard activities by converting so much of his property to wildlife. There are more than two dozen raised beds for vegetables, each 35 to 50 feet long. The substantial wildlife population in the vicinity does not cause much problem, although any corn grown is generally lost to the squirrels.

Future plans for the property include the addition of several pawpaw trees. Creekmore doesn't expect to get much, if any, fruit, but he is sure the raccoons will like it! He also plans to convert yet more lawn into a mulched area.

Flowers in various shades of red and pink, TOP and MIDDLE, as well as orange are highly attractive to butterflies and hummingbirds. BOTTOM, a well-planted mini-pond adds a completely different attraction to any backyard habitat, both for human eyes and wildlife needs.

SHRUBS ON THEIR OWN

HRUBS AND SMALL TREES don't have to be part of a hedgerow or thicket to have value to wildlife. Individual plants or clusters of them will provide food and cover, particularly when planted around the bases of trees. They are also useful in blending the buildings and fences of your property with the habitat features.

Traditional pruning techniques should be altered slightly to get the most wildlife value out of your shrubs. Although both thinning and cutting back have their benefits, the latter generally renders more wildlife benefit by producing bushier, denser areas of foliage.

Your pruning of these shrubs should no longer be aimed at producing neatly angled, uniform plants. Certainly trim the top and side shoots as you see fit. But allow the lower branches to grow right to the ground, or even encourage this by weighing down the lowest branches to train their growth downward. This greatly enhances the cover that they provide, especially for ground-nesting wildlife.

Before any pruning begins, be certain that you know which part of the shrub produces blossoms and fruit. If they occur on new growth, you won't want to snip these portions of the plant in spring.

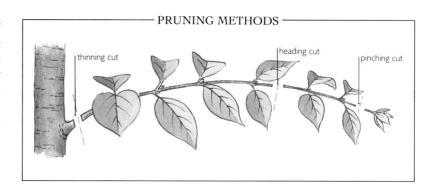

PRUNING METHODS

thinning cut
heading cut
pinching cut

BELOW: The berries of some common plants, like the pokeberry that this cedar waxwing is eating, are poisonous to humans but relished as food by many wildlife species.

ABOVE: Different pruning methods produce different results. Thinning gives a taller, more open plant; heading, a thicker, rounder plant with more branches; and pinching, an even thicker and rounder plant.

Native Shrubs to Benefit Wildlife

* D – Deciduous, C – Coniferous
**NE – Northeast, SE – Southeast, MW – Midwest, SW – Southwest, NW – Northwest, W – West

BOTANICAL NAME	COMMON NAME	HEIGHT (FT.)	PLANT TYPE*	REGIONS**
Amelanchier spp.	serviceberries	6–25	D	all
Arctostaphylos spp.	manzanitas	½–15	C	all
Beloperone californica	California beloperone	3–6	D	SW
Buddleia davidii	orange-eye butterfly bush	5–10	D	all
Chrysothamnus spp.	rabbitbrushes	1–7	D	SW NW
Cornus sericea	red-osier dogwood	4–8	D	NE MW NW
Gaultheria shallon	salal	18	C	NW
Gaylussacia brachycera	box huckleberry	½–1	C	NE
Ilex verticillata	winterberry	6–10	D	NE SE MW
Larrea tridentata	creosote bush	5–10	C	SW
Mahonia aquifolium	Oregon grape-holly	3–6	C	all
Myrica spp.	bayberries	12	D	all
Oemleria cerasiformis	osoberry	10–15	D	NW
Parthenocissus quinquefolia	Virginia creeper	–	D	NE SE MW
Prunus maritima	beach plum	6	D	NE
Prunus pumila	sand cherry	5	D	NE MW NW
Rhamnus crocea	redberry buckthorn	3–10	C	SW
Rhododendron catawbiense	catawba rhododendron	5–12	C	NE SE MW
Ribes spp.	currants	3–6	D	all
Rubus spp.	blackberries, raspberries	3–5	D	all
Sambucus canadensis	American elder	5–12	D	NE SE
Vaccinium spp.	blueberries	1–20	D	all
Viburnum dentatum	arrowwood viburnum	10	D	NE SE
Viburnum prunifolium	blackhaw viburnum	8–20	D	NE SE MW
Viburnum trilobum	American cranberry bush viburnum	8–12	D	NE MW NW

TRANSPLANTING A TREE

trench

burlap

rollers

ABOVE: Caring for the roots must be the utmost concern in moving a tree. To lessen impact on the plant, keep the ball of soil about the roots intact throughout the move. Apply a burlap wrap around the soil before the move.

THE IMPORTANCE OF TREES

TREES ARE ESSENTIAL FOR many of the most popular backyard wildlife species. Conifers provide excellent cover for wildlife even during the tough winter periods of snow, ice, and bitter winds, as well as some food in their cones. They also grow relatively quickly. Deciduous trees, on the other hand, provide less cover over a shorter period of the year, but give substantially more food value in their fruits, nuts, seeds, and berries. Provide both types of trees for maximum wildlife benefit.

With enough financing, large trees are available for a quick start. But for most of us trees are a long-term project, taking years to develop to maturity. If you are starting without any mature trees, you may want to plant your first ones along the perimeter of your property. This will give a clear definition to your efforts.

Shrubs, which grow much faster, can be planted in front of the new trees, to "fill in" for them until they reach a stage of growth where they are useful to wildlife.

If you have mature trees on your property – especially those that produce wildlife food – cherish them. Whenever possible, plan all your other enhancements around them. Add to them with smaller, shade-tolerant species.

DEAD AND DYING TREES

Our love affair with mature trees should continue even beyond their deaths. Snags are dead or partially dead and often partially hollow trees that are still standing, and are another element of the backyard habitat likely to attract both wildlife and community complaint. And the bigger the snag, the more of both it probably will attract.

Unless a snag poses a threat to safety, keep it in place. To the un-initiated eye, it may appear to be a useless eyesore, but many species of wildlife see it as a valuable – even essential – source of shelter and food.

We refer to those creatures that give birth to and nurture their young in upright openings, such as those found in snags, as cavity nesters. There are many of them, ranging from squirrels to many bird species that are much sought after by backyard habitatters.

The dying wood of the snag attracts many insects to lay their eggs there. In turn, these eggs and the hatching larvae attract birds such as woodpeckers and nuthatches. Mushrooms and other fungi may grow on moist areas of the wood, creating a favored food source for squirrels and chipmunks.

If you have no snags on your property, you may be able to make one out of a tree you need to remove. Trees can cause problems in your backyard. The invasive roots of one may threaten a drainage or septic system. Weak-

Whether alive or dead, trees are a major wildlife habitat element. RIGHT: Living trees provide nesting space for birds and other creatures such as squirrels, plus a ready supply of nutrient-filled mulch each fall. Nut-producing trees have an added food value. LEFT: Rotting stumps, logs, and standing snags are food-producing, breeding areas for insects and mushrooms. These in turn are important food for many species of wildlife. A hollowed stump, filled with some rich soil, can also provide an unusual planter for some wildflowers and wild grasses.

NICHES FOR LIVING

ZONE 5

tree canopy

ZONE 4

mature shrubs and
young trees

ZONE 3

young and short shrubs

ZONE 2

seedlings, taller grasses and weeds
grasses and weeds

ZONE 1

soil and subsoil

LEFT: Every fully functioning natural environment offers a range of vertical niches. Each niche supports a different array of wildlife. Shown here are the niches of a typical eastern forest.

ABOVE: Trees also can be beautiful elements of your habitat landscape. In addition to food and shelter considerations, think ahead to fall colors and the eventual canopy spread of the mature tree.

wooded or disease-prone trees may be more trouble than they are worth. A crowded group of trees may need to be thinned out. A tree might shade or compete unfavorably with a more desirable tree. Lightning or strong winds may have damaged it, creating a safety hazard. You might want to consider converting such a problem tree, if it is between 6 and 20 inches in diameter, into a snag.

Simply girdle the tree by removing a 4-inch-wide belt of outer and inner barks around the trunk. Eventually, the tree will die and, within a few years, decay will bring the wood to the proper consistency for feeding and nesting.

After a snag falls to the ground, all of these benefits continue. Some individual species that make use of the log (which the snag becomes on contact with the ground) may change, but the great attraction for a diversity of species will continue. For example, the hollow will no longer provide nesting for most birds, but ground-dwelling species such as rabbits, opossums, and skunks may now find their birthing space there. And the rotting log and the ground beneath will soon attract an array of creatures, such as salamanders, that inhabit a limited range of habitats.

Of course, if snags are not an option on your property, artificial snags – better known as birdhouses – will attract many of the same cavity-nesting creatures. These are covered on page 94.

COST-REDUCING SHELTER BELTS

Trees and bushes have benefits for the homeowner beyond all their substantial powers to attract wildlife. According to research at Pennsylvania State University, shelter belts of trees and bushes have reduced home heating costs by 10–25 percent. These shelter belts include windbreaks for reducing the effects of winter winds and branching deciduous trees for shade from the hot summer sun.

The Penn State studies determined that the optimum placement of a windbreak should be upwind from the home five times the mature height of the trees. For example, if you expect the trees to be 10 feet tall at maturity, you should plant them 50 feet upwind of the home. The rows also should be 50 feet wider than the home at both ends.

Although trees have captured most of the publicity for their fall colors, many other plants also produce remarkable autumn colors. Many vines, like the Virginia creeper *(Parthenocissus quinquifolia)*, ABOVE, and shrubs, like the sumac, *(Rhus* spp.), BELOW, generate colors to rival any tree. Both of these species provide quality food for wildlife, as well as the added landscape feature of layering in different colors at different heights.

Native Trees to Benefit Wildlife

* D – Deciduous, C – Coniferous
**NE – Northeast, SE – Southeast, MW – Midwest, SW – Southwest, NW – Northwest, W – West

BOTANICAL NAME	COMMON NAME	HEIGHT (FT.)	PLANT TYPE*	REGIONS**
Acer rubrum	red maple	40–60	D	all
Alnus rubra	red alder	35–40	D	NW
Arbutus arizonica	madrone	20–50	C	SW
Carya illinoiensis	pecan	65–95	D	SE MW
Carya spp.	hickories	50–80	D	NE SE
Celtis spp.	hackberries	8–20	D	all
Cornus florida	flowering dogwood	10–30	D	NE SE
Diospyros virginiana	common persimmon	30–60	D	NE SE
Elaeagnus angustifolia	Russian olive	15–30	D	all
Fagus grandifolia	American beech	40–70	D	NE SE MW
Fraxinus americana	white ash	50–80	D	NE SE MW
Ilex opaca	American holly	40–50	C	NE SE
Juniperus scopulorum	Rocky Mountain juniper	30–40	C	all
Juniperus virginiana	eastern red cedar	40–55	C	all
Malus spp.	crab apples, apples	30	D	all
Morus alba	white mulberry	30–50	D	all
Nyssa sylvatica	black tupelo	30–50	D	NE SE
Olneya tesota	ironwood	15–25	C	SW
Picea pungens	Colorado spruce	30–60	C	all
Pinus ponderosa	ponderosa pine	55–95	C	all
Pinus strobus	eastern white pine	50–75	C	all
Pinus taeda	loblolly pine	35–50	C	SE MW SW
Platanus wrightii	sycamore	35–80	D	SW
Populus tremuloides	quaking aspen	30–50	D	all
Prosopis juliflora	mesquite	20–50	D	SW
Prunus serotina	wild black cherry	40–60	D	all
Prunus virginiana	chokecherry	20–35	D	all
Pseudotsuga menziesii	Douglas fir	40–70	C	NE MW NW
Quercus alba	white oak	50–80	D	NE SE MW
Quercus gambelii	gambel oak	20–40	D	SW
Quercus palustris	pin oak	50–70	D	NE SE MW
Quercus phellos	willow oak	30–60	D	NE SE MW
Quercus rubra	red oak	60–75	D	NE SE MW
Sorbus aucuparia	European mountain ash	20–45	D	NE MW NW
Tsuga canadensis	Canada hemlock	40–70	C	NE MW NW

ABOVE: Evergreens provide maximum shelter from the elements during all seasons, but are most beneficial during hard winter storms and extremely cold temperatures. They also are a haven for nesting birds in the spring.

BELOW: Snags – standing dead or dying trees – are packed with wildlife-attracting power. Many species, like this red-headed woodpecker, find both their insect food and their nesting spots in these trees.

WATER IS CRUCIAL

WATER IS THE NECESSITY most often overlooked by homeowners wanting to attract wildlife into their backyards. Unfortunately for them, this element that most of us take for granted is an amazing lure for nearly all forms of life.

Drinking to relieve thirst is the most obvious need fulfilled by whatever water you provide. While many wildlife species get sufficient water from the foods they eat, few will pass up the chance for a long, quenching drink.

The second use, bathing, is more important to many species – particularly birds – than initially you might suppose. In order of importance, birds' reasons for bathing seem to be cleansing the feathers of dirt and parasites, offsetting the discomfort of new feather growth, and cooling.

Some birds, such as the American robin, starlings, and various grackle species, attack the water with a fluttering, quivering relish. Others, such as mourning doves, are quite calm in their bathing, landing in the water, taking a drink, and then just standing there for long periods. Flycatchers and swallows never actually settle into the water; instead, they dive bomb repeatedly to slice the water's surface with their breasts and return to their perch for additional preening.

A third use of water for some wildlife species is best described as lifestyle preference. The raccoon is our best example of this. It's a myth that the masked bandit must wash

Plants for In and Around the Backyard Pond

* These cattails, rushes, and sedges are generally grown along the edges of the pond in the wetland conditions created there. They form a distinctive border around the water, but they are very invasive. Their spread needs to be limited with barrier strips and by removing their seed heads immediately after the first frost.

BOTANICAL NAME	COMMON NAME	FLOWER COLOR	HEIGHT (IN.)	WATER DEPTH OVER CROWN (IN.)	USDA HARDINESS ZONES
Acorus calamus*	sweet flag	NA	to 30	to 6	4–10
Alternanthera reinekkii	scarlet alternanthera	NA	to 18	to 12	9–10
Anubias lanceolata	Africa crypt	NA	to 12	to 12	10
Cabomba caroliniana	Carolina fanwort	NA	to 15	to 24	6–10
Caltha palustris	marsh marigold	yellow	to 12	to 4	2–5
Canna spp.	cannas	yellow, red	to 48	to 4	7–10
Ceratophyllum demersum	hornwort	NA	to 36	to 48	5–10
Colocasia esculenta	taro	NA	to 40	to 8	8–10
Crinum americanum	bog lily	blue-white	to 24	to 6	8–10
Cyperus alternifolius*	umbrella plant	NA	to 60	to 6	8–10
Cyperus haspan	dwarf papyrus	NA	to 30	to 6	8–10
Cyperus minima	dwarf cyperus	NA	to 18	to 6	8–10
Echinodorus cordifolius	radicans swordplant	NA	to 30	to 12	8–10
Eleocharis montevidensis*	spike rush	NA	to 12	to 12	6–10
Elodea canadensis	anacharis	white	to 36	to 30	5–10
Hemigraphis colorata	purple waffle plant	NA	to 12	to 10	9–10
Hydrocleys nymphoides	water poppy	yellow	4–12	4–12	9–10
Hydrocotyle vulgaris	pennywort	NA	to 18	to 12	8–10
Iris fulva	red iris	red	to 24	to 6	5–9
Iris pseudacorus	yellow flag	yellow	to 30	to 12	4–9
Iris siberica	Siberian iris	violet	to 30	to 4	3–9
Iris versicolor	blue iris	blue	to 30	to 6	4–9
Ludwigia natans	red ludwigia	NA	to 18	to 12	8–10
Myriophyllum spp.	myriophyllums	NA	to 24	to 24	4–10
Nymphaea spp.	water lilies	variable	to surface	to 18	1–10
Nymphoides peltata	floating heart	yellow	4–12	4–12	6–10

BOTANICAL NAME	COMMON NAME	COLOR	HEIGHT	DEPTH	ZONE
Peltandra sagittaefolia	white arum	white	to 18	to 6	5–10
Peltandra virginica	water arum	yellow	to 24	to 6	5–9
Pontederia cordata	pickerel weed	blue, white	to 30	to 12	3–9
Sagittaria spp.	arrowheads	white	to 24	to 12	5–10
Saururus cernuus	lizard's tail	NA	to 18	to 6	4–9
Spathiphyllum floribundum	peace lily	white	to 15	to 3	9–10
Typha latifolia*	cattail	NA	to 84	to 12	2–10
Typha minima*	dwarf cattail	NA	to 48	to 12	3–10
Vallisneria spp.	eel grasses	NA	to 24	to 24	4–10

everything before eating it, but raccoons do spend a great deal of time in any water they come across. Their typical behavior is shallow wading with active feeling about the pebbles and debris on the bottom.

And, finally, there is a large group of wildlife that spends all or part of its life in the water. Your backyard habitat simply will not attract or support them without an adequate water source. Fish are obviously one such group of animals. But ground-level water is similarly essential for many reptiles and amphibians, such as many species of frogs, turtles, and salamanders. Such small bodies of water also offer the chance for attracting wading birds that would otherwise never frequent the backyard.

CHOOSING AND SITING YOUR WATER SOURCE

Given their importance in the backyard habitat, water sources are amazingly easy to provide. They can range from the traditional bird bath all the way to a large pond or stream complete with a bordering wetland.

Bird baths are available in a wide variety of designs. Cement or pottery are the most durable materials. Pedestals of at least 3 feet in height provide bathing birds with greater security from ground-based predators, like cats. Water depth should range to no more than 3 inches. Sides should be rough to provide secure footing.

Nearly any water-holding container can be sunk into the ground as a ready-made pool. But whatever form you choose, it should have a variety of depths. These should range from a flat area of $1/2$-inch-deep water – or gently sloping from $1/2$ inch to 3 inches – to at least 2 feet at the center, if you plan to add plants and fish. The shallow portions will provide for the preferences of bathing birds and prevent drowning deaths for a wide range of species. Additional shallow areas and islands should be

ABOVE: Any water source you can provide will repay you many times over with the variety of wildlife it attracts. The traditional pedestal-type bird baths have been around for generations because they serve their purpose well, but many more options are opened with the installation of an in-ground mini-pond.

provided at various spots across the water source, if it is large enough to warrant these extras.

Location of your water source, whatever its design, is of paramount importance. A flower-encircled pond, bird bath, or fountain may seem to be the perfect centerpiece for the lawn. But from wildlife's perspective, adjacent cover – shrubs, trees, rocks – are the more important concern.

Protection and escape potential from predators and the elements while drinking and bathing are critical to most wildlife species. When they are engaged in these activities, many species are as exposed as they ever let themselves become; for example, consider the bathing bird with waterlogged feathers trying for a quick escape from a stalking cat.

Perhaps a corner of the backyard, just a few feet from a hedge or brush pile and with closely overhanging tree branches, is the optimum location. The hedge or brush pile should be close enough for a quick escape but not for pouncing by predators. Of course, if this can be provided at the center of the yard, I can think of no better accent to the overall environment for both you and the wild creatures.

On the site you've chosen, mark off the shape of the pond that you want to have. This might be dictated for you if you plan to purchase a pre-fabricated plastic or concrete pond liner. An irregular shape, rather than round, square, or triangular, will give the pond a more natural look.

Regardless of design and location, nothing you do with your water source will prove more attractive to wildlife than adding running water. The splashing sound is a real magnet for birds and mammals. This might be as simple as a jug of water or a catchment system suspended over the source, with a tiny hole in the bottom that constantly allows water droplets to splash onto the water's surface.

ABOVE: A mini-pond with a shallow, gradually sloping, nonslip bottom is most appreciated by birds, which prefer depths of 2 inches or less for bathing and drinking.

For a more natural-looking system, place a simple recirculating pump in a naturally camouflaged enclosure next to the water source to draw water from the bottom of the source and deposit it back at the surface. Direct the recirculated water over a few rocks or down a waterfall before re-entering the source.

If your water source is a pond, you will want to introduce plants and animals. After filling your pond, wait for several days so the chemicals that are added to tap water – chlorine and fluoride – can escape.

When this waiting period has passed, it is generally a good idea to add a few quarts of water from a local pond that supports a healthy amount of animal life. Include a bit of the mud and muck from the bottom of that pond as well. This will jump-start your mini-pond with a fully functioning ecosystem of the myriad life forms that occupy such water.

ADD SOME PLANTS

Plants will add yet another dimension to your water source. Their addition soon raises a simple mini-pond to the level of an aquatic community. Snails, frogs, and many insects will naturally follow their introduction.

Some pond-keepers place several inches of rich soil on the bottom of their ponds, in which they then plant. However, this method will cause initial, and sometimes continuing, cloudiness in the water. It also encourages algae blooms and premature eutrophication of the pond.

A note about water clarity is

appropriate here. The water in your water source is healthy, living water – not intended for human drinking, bathing, or swimming. As such, it should not be crystal clear. The cloudy, greenish appearance tells us that the millions of tiny plants and animals that should be present are floating there.

However, such water sources can and do become too murky. Nature's mechanism for dealing with this situation is the freshwater mussel, which constantly filters the water for food and in the process cleans it. Several of these shellfish will soon have the water back to a healthy state. A filter in the recirculating system will accomplish the same feat.

All of these problems can be largely avoided by planting in individual containers, with the soil held in place by a top dressing of gravel. Such "container-gardening" also allows much greater flexibility in placement and re-placement of the plants and in cleaning the pond.

Most backyard ponds will be small and self-contained. Therefore it is not as important to restrict your water plant choices to native species. The accompanying table will help you make your selections.

After adding the plants, several more days must pass to allow the water temperature and chemistry to stabilize before adding fish and other animals. The species mentioned earlier will generally find your pond on their own. There may even come a time when you find a fish species or two that you did not introduce. Fish are commonly transported to new waters in egg form stuck to the legs of birds. But you will see faster results if you add the fish yourself.

Many exotic species are available through pet shops and garden centers, but for many backyard habitatters, native species have a special appeal. The state agency with responsibility for fish resources must be consulted before natives are stocked.

BELOW: With enough space and resources, an elaborate water source can be developed as a special centerpiece within the backyard habitat. The ornamental and human-use factors need not be sacrificed for wildlife purposes, as water holds a similar appeal for humans, too.

MIDWEST GARDEN

TECHNICALLY SPEAKING, MARY TAIT'S (ABOVE) HOME IN THE ROUTE 1 SECTION AROUND LINCOLN, NEBRASKA, IS PART OF A DEVELOPMENT (LIKE MOST OF THE OTHER BACKYARD HABITATS DESCRIBED IN THIS BOOK); IN HER NEIGHBORHOOD THE PARCELS OF LAND RANGE FROM 3 TO 4 ACRES. HER OWN PROPERTY IS 10 ACRES; THE ORIGINAL 5 ACRES WHERE THE HOME WAS FIRST BUILT, AND A FURTHER 5 ACRES PURCHASED LATER FOR PROTECTION AGAINST ENCROACHING DEVELOPMENT.

Neighbors display varying attitudes toward their properties: Two mow every square inch, one forgoes mowing on a telephone line easement, two allow some of their back acreage to grow wild, several use much of their ground for livestock and leave it unmowed, and another allows the wild growth to take hold between the trees he planted for windbreaks. Wherever unmowed acreage exists in the area, ring-necked pheasants and quail have taken up residence.

Tait, on the other hand, leaves much of her property in as wild a

On the reverting farmland that is Mary Tait's Nebraska backyard, many native species of wildflower have taken hold, such as the hardy prairie sunflower, TOP, and the ironweed, ABOVE. Both are highly attractive to many bird and insect species. Nearly any site in North America, if left to its own devices, will sport a growth of native plants, within the first year of such an effort.

state as possible. She even encourages the critters to make use of her various outbuildings. For example, she leaves the shutters on the barn windows open so barn swallows can nest inside, which they do atop the light fixtures. Opossums, too, have been known to spend a chilly night in the barn's warmth.

Similarly, she never sprays the fruit trees on the property, choosing instead to allow the wildlife full and unpolluted access to the five apple trees and the plum thicket.

Tait's property doesn't offer any natural source of water, but she compensates for this with two pedestal bird baths, two rubberized tubs at ground level, and an inch-deep, busboy-type tray filled with water. The water provides a welcome respite for many species of birds, but she has also seen other creatures stopping for a drink.

She didn't always make water available for wildlife. But, when a frog "moved in," attracted by the water pans she set out for her dogs, she saw the wildlife value in the practice. Now, she even places a pan under a dripping faucet. She also wets an open area of ground to create mud for those birds that use it for nest building. Future plans include establishing a plate of mud, which will be easier to keep filled.

"As you watch, you see what they need and what they utilize." So Tait explains the various adaptations that she's created over the years. When she moved here in December 1972, the property had no trees. The new development was on the site of old farmland and

LEFT: Even plants, like this birch tree, that at first glance appear to provide little for wildlife, in fact offer items like edible buds.

whatever the farmer had left standing, the developers removed. "They mowed down everything when they developed this area. They thought it made it more presentable."

A great deal of work has gone into reversing those "improvements." Brush piles have been created from trimmings left on the property. As some planted trees have died they've been left standing as snags; although they aren't large enough for cavity nesters to utilize, they certainly do provide a ready source of insects in their rotting wood.

One problem that Tait encountered as she attracted birds onto the property was collisions with windows in the house. Happily, these were rarely fatal. She simply placed the stunned birds in a cage until they seemed fully revived, and then released them again. Nevertheless, she installed hawk silhouettes on the windows to prevent further collisions.

Based on her experiences with wildlife in the backyard, Tait's advice to the would-be wildlife gardener is: "Talk to someone who's been doing it for a while in your area to find out how it works. It takes a lot of time to see what the birds go for and what they like. Input from someone with experience can cut this learning curve substantially."

cottontail rabbit

BELOW: This maple tree is nearly ready to drop its crop of seeds for the year. This event will spark a great deal of feeding activity among a wide variety of bird and mammal species. The same tree will provide food in the spring, when its buds appear, and in the summer, when sap runs out of any wounds or breaks in the bark.

Some of the wildlife-attracting plants found in the Tait habitat:

TREES
apple, cedar, chokecherry, cottonwood, crab apple, elm, locust, maple, mulberry, plum. (Note: many of the plum and elm trees are grown in dense thickets which provide excellent shelter.)

SHRUBS AND VINES
autumn olive, blackberry, currant, hawthorn, mulberry, red osier dogwood

FLOWERS AND HERBS
alfalfa, buffalo berry, clover, daisy, goldenrod, ironweed, milkweed, orchard grass, raspberry, snowberry, thistle, wildflower (various species), wild grass (various species), wild sunflower

Some of the wildlife sighted in the Tait habitat:

BIRDS
American goldfinch, American robin, barn swallow, black-capped chickadee, blue jay, brown thrasher, chimney swift, common flicker, common grackle, cowbird, dickcissel, eastern bluebird, European starling, finch (various species), gray catbird, hawk (various species), junco, killdeer, kingbird, loggerhead shrike, meadowlark, mourning dove, northern cardinal, northern mockingbird, northern oriole, quail, red-breasted nuthatch, ring-necked pheasant, rufous-sided towhee, song sparrow, tree sparrow, sparrow (various species), white-breasted nuthatch

MAMMALS
cottontail rabbit, coyote, opossum, raccoon, red fox, white-tailed deer

REPTILES AND AMPHIBIANS
bull snake, garter snake, king snake

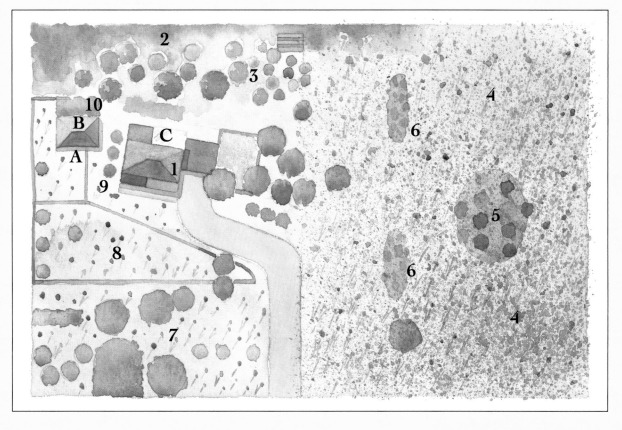

TAIT HABITAT
1 House, garage and driveway, yard
2 mixed trees
3 platform and bench amid thick
growth of mixed trees
4 wildflowers
5 thicket of plums and elms

6 goldenrod
7 wildflowers with scattered trees and
thickets of plum and locust
8 pole fence around wildflowers,
cedars, and elms
9 locust trees, wildflowers
10 cottonwood

A roosting boxes in barn
B stack of straw bales in barn used by
rabbits, foxes, and possums
C water and food for birds

Every inch of a backyard habitat does
not have to be committed entirely to
wildlife uses. However, most backyard
pursuits will bring some wildlife
benefit, unintended though it may be.
For example, a moonflower planted
purely for ornamental purposes, FAR
LEFT, provides nectar for moths.
Invaders such as milkweed, LEFT, are
also attractive to wildlife.

BETWEEN LAND AND WATER

SOME PROPERTY OWNERS ARE reluctant to add much of a water source to their backyards because of the potential for adding to a problem they've already been fighting since they bought the property – low-lying wet spots that never seem to dry completely, regardless of rainfall totals.

These can be costly and frustrating areas to deal with, and an in-ground water source will likely create a wet area around its perimeter. However, in the backyard habitat, the goal need not be to bring the troublesome spot into compliance with the rest of the property. In fact, such wet areas present unique opportunities to provide yet another habitat element.

Although the term *wetland* generally applies to larger expanses than will be feasible in the backyard, we are, in effect, discussing mini-wetlands here. And, even a cursory reading of newspaper headlines over the past few years will probably have left you with an impression of just how crucial this form of habitat really is.

Wetlands are among the most productive natural ecosystems. Their food-producing capabilities rival any agricultural fields or orchards of similar size. They are home to many species of wildlife and plants that can't live elsewhere. They provide a proportion of the habitat needs of other species.

Of course, your mini-wetland will be much more limited in scope than these amazing natural systems, unless you have much more

Plants for Wetland Areas

* C – Coniferous tree, D – Deciduous tree, G – Grass, O – Other, S – Shrub, W – Wildflower
** NE – Northeast, SE – Southeast, MW – Midwest, SW – Southwest, NW – Northwest, W – West

BOTANICAL NAME	COMMON NAME	FLOWER COLOR	HEIGHT (IN.)	TYPE*	REGIONS**
Abies balsamea	balsam fir	NA	40–60 (ft.)	C	NE MW
Acer rubrum	red maple	NA	to 92 (ft.)	D	NE SE MW
Agropyron trachycaulum	slender wheatgrass	NA	18	G	NW SW W
Ammi majus	bishop's flower	white	to 36	W	all
Anemone canadensis	meadow anemone	white	12–24	W	NE MW
Artemisia lactiflora	white mugwort	white	36–48	W	NE MW
Aruncus dioicus	goat's beard	white	to 72	W	all
Asclepias incarnata	swamp milkweed	pink	to 48	W	all
Aster ericoides	heath aster	white	24–36	W	NE MW
Aster novae-angliae	New England aster	varies	48–72	W	NE MW
Astilbe spp.	astilbes	varies	12–36	W	NE MW NW
Betula alleghaniensis	yellow birch	NA	32–72 (ft.)	D	NE
Betula papyrifera	paper birch	NA	to 30 (ft.)	D	NE
Calamagrostis canadensis	bluejoint reedgrass	NA	36	G	all
Caltha palustris	marsh marigold	yellow	6–12	W	all
Camassia quamash	common camas	blue	12–18	W	NW W
Carex spp.	sedges	NA	12–36	O	all
Castilleja spp.	paintbrushes	varies	12–14	W	NW SW W
Cephalanthus occidentalis	buttonbush	yellow-green	to 15 (ft.)	S	all
Chelone glabra	white turtlehead	NA	to 72	O	NE MW
Claytonia virginica	spring beauty	pink	4–6	W	NE SE MW SW
Cornus sericea	red-osier dogwood	white	to 8 (ft.)	S	all
Deschampsia cespitosa	tufted hairgrass	NA	36	G	NW SW W
Digitalis purpurea	foxglove	red, pink, purple, yellow, white	24–48	W	all
Drosera spp.	sundews	various	4–6	W	MW NW
Echinacea purpurea	purple coneflower	purple	24–36	W	all

BOTANICAL NAME	COMMON NAME	COLOR	HEIGHT	TYPE*	REGIONS**
Epilobium angustifolium	fireweed	pink-red	12–72	W	all
Eupatorium maculatum	Joe-pye weed	pink-purple	to 72	W	NE SE MW SW
Eupatorium perfoliatum	boneset	white	36–48	W	NE MW
Filipendula ulmaria	queen-of-the-meadow	white	to 72	W	NE MW
Fraxinus nigra	black ash	NA	to 65 (ft.)	D	NE
Glyceria striata	fowl mannagrass	NA	24	G	NE MW
Helenium autumnale	sneezeweed	yellow, orange	24–48	W	all
Helianthus annuus	common sunflower	yellow	36–96	W	all
Heracleum mantegazzianum	giant hogweed	white	to 72	W	NE MW NW
Iris ensata	Japanese iris	purple	to 36	W	all
Iris pseudacorus	yellow flag	yellow	to 60	W	NE MW NW
Iris sibirica	Siberian iris	varies	to 36	W	MW NW
Iris versicolor	blue flag	blue	24–36	W	NE SE MW
Juncus spp.	rushes	varies	7–30	O	all
Kalmia angustifolia	sheep laurel	pink, red	to 36	S	NE SE
Kalmia latifolia	mountain laurel	pink, white	to 18 (ft.)	S	NE SE
Ligularia hodgsonii	Hodgson's ligularia	orange	to 36	W	MW NW
Lobelia cardinalis	cardinal flower	red	to 36	W	NE MW
Lobelia siphilitica	great blue lobelia	blue	to 36	W	all
Lysimachia clethroides	gooseneck loosestrife	white	36–48	W	NE MW NW
Lythrum virgatum	loosestrife	purple	to 72	W	NE MW
Mentha aquatica	water mint	lavender	to 24	W	all
Mertensia virginica	Virginia bluebells	blue	8–24	W	NE MW NW
Mimulus guttatus	common monkey flower	yellow	to 24	W	NE MW NW
Monarda didyma	bee balm	red	to 48	W	all
Monarda fistulosa	wild bergamot	lavender	to 48	W	all
Myosotis sylvatica	garden forget-me-not	blue	6–15	W	all
Pedicularis groenlandica	elephant-heads	pink	6–24	W	NW SW W
Peltiphyllum peltatum	umbrella plant	pink	to 60	W	all
Penstemon digitalis	foxglove penstemon	white	to 48	W	NE SE MW SW W
Petasites japonicus	butterbur	yellow	to 72	W	all *(continued)*

available space than the average backyard. But even an area of 100 square feet will add a surprising diversity to your habitat. And if you're fortunate enough to have property that borders on a brook, stream, river, pond, lake, or other body of water, like an in-ground water source you created, your possibilities are virtually limitless.

A mini-wetland is not at all difficult to get started. First of all, cease all efforts to drain the site. You might even want to remove any pipes, tiles, or the like that have been installed to that end. If you don't have such a problem spot in your backyard, one can usually be created simply by making a depression.

Before doing anything else, check with your state environmental agencies for wetlands regulations. Most states have enacted fairly strict laws in recent years. You may be surprised to find that some of your previous efforts at draining the site may now be in violation of these laws.

Generally your backyard soil can use some enhancement to become an optimum wetland base. A few bags of peat moss, top soil, and loam mixed together and spread over the site will give it the boost it needs. If the soil in your wetland site is similar to that in the rest of your yard, you might want to replace some of it with more of the above mixture. On the other hand, if your soil is black and rich, you probably won't want to disturb it at all as this is normal wetland soil and needs no help.

ABOVE: Marsh marigold (*Caltha palustris*) is one of the many species that thrive in a wetland setting, making it a good choice for the area immediately surrounding an in-ground water source. An area does not need to be large and expansive to be considered a wetland in the backyard habitat.

BOTANICAL NAME	COMMON NAME	COLOR	HEIGHT	TYPE*	REGIONS**
Phragmites communis	common reed	NA	to 96	O	all
Picea mariana	black spruce	NA	75–90 (ft.)	C	NE MW
Pinguicula spp.	butterworts	purple	to 72	W	NE MW
Polygonum affine	knotweed	pink	to 18	W	NE MW NW
Polygonum bistorta	snakeweed	blue	to 24	W	NE MW NW
Pontederia cordata	pickerelweed	blue	to 48	W	all
Primula japonica	Japanese primrose	yellow	to 24	W	all
Rhododendron spp.	rhododendrons	varies	to 10 (ft.)	S	all
Rodgersia aesculifolia	fingerleaf rodgersia	white	to 48	W	NE SE MW NW SW
Rudbeckia hirta	black-eyed Susan	yellow	24–36	W	all
Sagittaria latifolia	arrowhead	white	to 48	W	all
Salix exigua	sandbar willow	NA	to 26 (ft.)	D	NE MW NW
Sarracenia spp.	pitcher plants	varies	to 30	W	NE MW
Solidago spp.	goldenrods	yellow	24–72	W	all
Symplocarpus foetidus	skunk cabbage	yellow	to 48	W	all
Telekia speciosa	oxeye daisy	yellow	to 36	W	all
Thalictrum aquilegifolium	meadow rue	varies	to 36	W	all
Thalictrum polygamum	king-of-the-meadow	white	to 96	W	NE MW NW
Tradescantia virginiana	spiderwort	purple, white	12–24	W	all
Trollius europaeus	globeflower	yellow	to 36	W	all
Tsuga canadensis	Canada hemlock	NA	to 110 (ft.)	C	NE MW
Typha spp.	cattails	NA	to 84	O	all
Vaccinium spp.	blueberries	varies	to 48	S	NE MW
Veratrum viride	false hellebore	yellow	to 48	W	NE MW
Verbena hastata	blue vervain	blue	to 60	W	NE MW
Vernonia noveboracensis	New York ironweed	purple	to 72	W	all
Veronicastrum virginicum	Culver's root	white	to 72	W	NE MW NW
Viola cornuta	horned violet	yellow and purple	5–8	W	all

Your next step is the establishment of plants. Your selection, of course, will vary from one region to the next. Some native species that you might consider are listed in the accompanying table.

Planting and maintenance will be your final steps. Wildlife will be quick to volunteer for the habitat you've created. That's how valuable wetlands of just about any size are.

BEACH AND DUNE AS SPECIAL CIRCUMSTANCES

RESIDENTS ALONG THE coasts needn't despair of being able to establish wildlife habitats like those described through much of this book. Coastal shorelines – beach, dune, rocks – may be unique environments, but they are anything but lacking in life.

Every wave dumps a new feast ashore to a waiting horde of wildlife. Shorebirds, such as plovers and gulls, dart about snagging one succulent bit after another. Crustaceans draw the water down to their buried mouths to siphon out their share. Others of their ilk, such as mole crabs, scurry across the sand devouring whatever tiny edibles they encounter. At night they are joined by mammals, such as red foxes, raccoons, and skunks, and even more crustaceans.

Just a bit farther inland, where grasses and shrubs cover the dunes, land-based wildlife begins to carve out its niches. Insects find a rich environment here, as do some reptiles and amphibians. Small mammals, such as rabbits and voles, and many songbirds are often abundant here. Their abundance in turn attracts the attention of hunters, such as hawks, owls, and red foxes.

Rocky, surf-pounded shorelines likewise have their array of wildlife. Shore and sea birds will be the most in evidence during periods of high tide. But, as the tide goes out, a myriad of small fish, shellfish, other crustaceans, seaweeds, and the like will be revealed in the many crevices, tidal pools, and other retaining points. Many additional bird species join in the feast that the retreating tide leaves behind, and mammals emerge into the night. The rocky cliffs overhead provide protected nesting sites for many species of birds.

The critical element on a sandy beach or dune area is the plant life. The plants hold everything else in place and build the environment by collecting and holding additional bits of sand as the wind carries them along. Some of the plants that do best in this environment are listed in the table on page 60.

After the plant life, which is needed to form the habitat, fresh water will do more to attract wildlife than anything else you can supply. Sources of truly fresh water can be extremely limited in this environment.

BELOW: The salt spray from the ocean, the brackish quality of most nearby inland water sources, the intense summer heat in the largely unshaded environment – these are just some of the unique challenges that face the backyard habitatter trying to develop the wildlife potential of a seaside property.

The water must be sheltered from the saline effect of the ocean – both the wave runoff and the salt spray. The former will completely foul the water, while the latter can taint it to the point of limiting its wildlife value. Locating the water source above the highest tide line will prevent runoff. A thick plant barrier or a slated roof to the seaside of the water source will protect it from most of the salt spray.

SALT MARSHES

Salt marshes are another distinct coastal habitat. With one critical exception, much of what was discussed in our section on wetlands applies to these areas as well. That exception is the saline environment, with which every resident – plant or animal – must cope. Despite this factor, salt marshes are some of Earth's most life-rich environments. They are a transitional environment of sorts, combining the elements of land and sea, and of saltwater and freshwater. For this reason, wildlife from each of the environments that come together in salt marshes can be found here.

Many of the plants discussed in our sections on wetlands and water habitats will do fine at the edges of salt marshes, but some plants that are particularly well adapted to life in this specialized environment are listed in the accompanying table. Unless something in the local environment is very much amiss, most often you will not need to supplement the naturally occurring plant life in this rich habitat.

Plants for a Beach-Dune Environment

* G – Grass, M – Moss/Lichen, S – Shrub, T – Tree, V – Vine, W – Wildflower
** BD – Beach side of dunes, ID – Between dunes, SD – Land side of dunes, T – Thickets on or between dunes, and edge between dunes and next inland habitat type

BOTANICAL NAME	COMMON NAME	PLANT TYPE*	LOCATION**
Acer spp.	maples	T	T
Ammophila breviligulata	American beach grass	G	BD
Aralia nudicaulis	wild sarsaparilla	W	T
Arctostaphylos uva-ursi	evergreen bearberry	S	SD
Arenaria peploides	seabeach sandwort	G	BD
Artemisia stellerana	beach wormwood	S	BD
Baptisia tinctoria	wild indigo	S	SD
Chasmanthium latifolium	northern sea oats	G	BD
Chrysopsis graminifolia	golden aster	W	SD
Cladonia cristella	redcrest lichen	M	ID
Cladonia rangiferina	reindeer moss	M	SD
Elymus glaucus	blue Lyme grass	G	SD
Euphorbia polygonifolia	seaside spurge	W	BD
Hudsonia tomentosa	beach heather	W	SD
Ilex spp.	hollies	S	T
Lathyrus japonicus	beach pea	V	BD
Lonicera spp.	honeysuckles	V	T
Myrica spp.	bayberries	S	ID
Opuntia compressa	prickly pear cactus	S	SD
Pinus rigida	pitch pine	T	T
Pisolithus tinctorius	crowned earthstar	W	ID
Prunus maritima	beach plum	S	ID
Prunus spp.	cherries	ST	T
Quercus spp.	oaks	ST	T
Rumex acetosella	sheep sorrel	G	T
Sassafras albidum	sassafras	T	T
Solidago sempervirens	seaside goldenrod	W	BD
Usnea strigosa	old man's beard	G	ID

Plants for the Salt Marsh

BOTANICAL NAME	COMMON NAME	COAST
Agalinis maritima	seaside gerardia	East
Agrostis alba	redtop	West
Aster tenuifolius	saltmarsh aster	East
Atriplex patula	fat-hen saltbush	West
Baccharis halimifolia	eastern bacharris	East
Baccharis pilularis	coyote brush	West
Carex spp.	sedges	West
Cirsium palustre	marsh thistle	East
Convolvulus sepium	hedge bindweed	East
Cordylanthus maritimus	marsh bird's beak	West
Cordylanthus mollis	soft bird's beak	West
Cotula corenopifolia	brass buttons	West
Cuscuta salina	dodder	West
Deschampsia spp.	hairgrasses	West
Distichlis spicata	spikegrass	East and West
Festuca rubra	red fescue	East
Frakenia grandifolia	alkali heath	West
Fucus vesiculosus	rockweed	East
Glaux maritima	sea milkwort	East and West
Grindelia squarrosa	curlycup gumweed	West
Grindelia stricta	marsh gum plant	West
Heleocharis parvula	dwarf spikesedge	West
Hibiscus palustris	swamp rose mallow	East
Hordeum brachyantherum	meadow barley	West
Ilex glabra	inkberry	East
Ilex opaca	American holly	East
Ilex verticillata	winterberry	East
Iva frutescens	marsh elder	East
Juncus balticus	Baltic rush	West
Juncus gerardii	black grass	East
Juncus lesueurii	salt rush	West
Kosteletzkya virginica	seashore mallow	East
Limonium californicum	marsh rosemary	West
Limonium carolinianum	sea lavender	East
Myosurus minimus	least mousetail	West

(continued)

ABOVE: Grasses are a key habitat element in the salt marsh environment. They provide much of the available cover as well as a ready source of food for many wildlife species. Many plants common to this environment do equally well growing on land or in water.

BOTANICAL NAME	COMMON NAME	COAST
Oplopanax horridus	devil's club	West
Panicum virgatum	switchgrass	East
Phragmites spp.	reeds	East
Plantago maritima	seaside plantain	East and West
Potentilla pacifica	Pacific silverweed	West
Prunus maritima	beach plum	East
Puccinellia maritima	seashore alkali grass	East
Puccinellia phyganodes	creeping alkali grass	West
Quercus spp.	oaks	East
Rumex occidentalis	western dock	West
Ruppia maritima	ditch grass, widgeon grass	West and East
Sabatia stellaris	saltmarsh pink	East
Salicornia spp.	glassworts	East
Salicornia spp.	pickleweeds	West
Scirpus cernuus	low bulrush	West
Scirpus maritimus	seacoast bulrush	West
Scirpus robustus	saltmarsh bulrush	East and West
Scirpus validus	tule	West
Solidago sempervirens	seaside goldenrod	East
Spartina alterniflora	saltmarsh cordgrass	East
Spartina foliosa	Pacific cordgrass	West
Spartina patens	saltmeadow cordgrass	East
Spartina pectinata	slough grass	East
Spergularia canadensis	Canadian sand spurry	West
Spergularia marina	saltmarsh sand spurry	West
Stellaria calycantha	northern starwort	West
Suaeda spp.	sea blites	East
Teucrium canadense	wood sage	East
Trifolium wormskjoldii	cow clover	West
Triglochin maritima	seaside arrowgrass	East and West

ABOVE RIGHT: Shifting sand is a constant problem on the beach. But the same plants that provide food and shelter for wildlife will help to anchor the blowing sand into developing dunes.

RIGHT: Sea oats are common plants of the coastal environment. They are easy to encourage in backyard habitats found in these areas and provide ample supplies of food for a wide variety of wildlife species.

DESERT AS A SPECIAL CIRCUMSTANCE

NORTH AMERICA'S DESERTS are, for the most part, not the typical sand-drenched, plantless places that the word normally brings to mind. In fact, they are covered with plant life.

Nevertheless, water and cover are the two elements that will attract the most wildlife to a backyard habitat that incorporates a desert environment.

Much of our previous discussion of water sources can be applied in the desert, although you will face a nearly constant struggle to maintain your supply. As a great deal of desert wildlife activity is confined to the early morning and the night to avoid the sun, refilling the water source just before sunset and early in the morning will provide the most benefit to wildlife.

BELOW: Nearly all desert regions of North America present much more plant life than commonly associated with such environments. The wildlife species that inhabit the deserts obtain much of their daily water requirements from plants, but any actual water source will still act as a magnet.

Several decades ago, the California Fish and Game Department developed what is probably the most effective and inexpensive-to-operate means of maintaining a water supply in this environment. It is known as the gallinaceous guzzler, for the desert quail it was first designed to service.

An exposed, flat, shallow "apron" of concrete or plastic collects rainwater and directs it through pipes into an underground collecting pool, also of concrete or plastic. The collecting pool is sheltered from the heat of the sun in a "cave" created by a roof of varying sorts. A shed-type roof can be buried under a layer of soil and sand and even planted with native vegetation. One or two sides of this artificial cave are left open to shallow gullies that allow access by wildlife. The size of these openings, particularly the height, will determine which species can make use of the water source.

An amazing amount of water can be gathered with this device. For example, in a region that receives just 2 inches of rainfall per year, an apron of just 550 square feet will collect about 700 gallons annually.

An easy variation on the above design is simply to direct rainfall runoff from home and outbuilding rain gutters into the underground collecting pool.

Shelter in the desert environment involves the ground even more than the plants. Although large animals and most birds must rely on shade and protection

Plants for the Desert Environment

* C – Cactus, G – Grass, S – Shrub, T – Tree, W – Wildflower
** C – Cactus, S – Sagebrush

BOTANICAL NAME	COMMON NAME	PLANT*	DESERT**
Acacia constricta	whitethorn acacia	T	S
Acacia greggii	cat claw	S	C
Agropyron dasystachyum	thickspire wheatgrass	G	S
Agropyron smithii	western wheatgrass	G	S
Agropyron spicatum	slender wheatgrass	G	S
Allenrolfea occidentalis	iodine bush	S	S
Amelanchier alnifolia	Saskatoon serviceberry	S	S
Aristida longiseta	red threeawn	G	S
Artemisia spp.	artemisias	S	S
Astragalus spp.	milkvetches	W	S
Atriplex spp.	saltbushes	S	S
Baileya multiradiata	desert marigold	W	C
Balsamorhiza sagittata	arrowleaf balsamroot	W	S
Bouteloua gracilis	blue gramma grass	G	S
Bromus tectorum	cheatgrass brome	G	S
Buchloe dactyloides	buffalo grass	G	C
Calliandra eriophylla	fairy duster	W	C
Calochortus nuttallii	sego lily	W	S
Carnegiea gigantea	saguaro	C	C
Castilleja chromosa	desert paintbrush	W	S
Castilleja spp.	paintbrushes	W	S
Celtis pallida	desert hackberry	W	C
Cercidium floridum	palo verde	W	C
Cercidium microphyllum	foothill palo verde	W	C
Cereus schottii	senita	C	C
Chrysopsis villosa	hairy golden aster	W	S
Chrysothamnus nauseosus	gray rabbitbush	S	S
Chrysothamnus viscidiflorus	rubber rabbitbush	S	S
Coryphantha vivipara	spiny star	C	C
Dalea spinosa	smoke tree	S	C
Delphinium spp.	larkspurs	W	S
Echinocereus engelmannii	hedgehog cactus	C	C
Elymus glaucus	giant wild-rye	G	S
Elymus hystrix	bottlebrush squirreltail	G	S
Encelia farinosa	brittlebush	S	C
Ephedra spp.	mormon teas	W	S C
Eriogonum spp.	wild buckwheats	G	S
Ferocactus acanthodes	barrel cactus	C	C
Festuca idahoensis	Idaho fescue	G	S

BOTANICAL NAME	COMMON NAME	PLANT*	DESERT**
Fouquieria splendens	ocotillo	C	C
Gaillardia aristata	blanket flower	W	S
Hesperocallis undulata	desert lily	W	C
Hibiscus denudatus	pale face	W	C
Hilaria jamesii	galleta grass	G	S
Hordèum jubatum	foxtail barley	G	S
Ipomopsis aggregata	scarlet gilia	W	S
Koeleria macrantha	prairie junegrass	G	S
Larrea tridentata	creosote bush	S	C
Lemaireocereus thurberi	organ pipe cactus	C	C
Lupinus spp.	lupines	W	S
Malacothrix glabrata	desert dandelion	W	S
Opuntia acanthocarpa	buckthorn cholla	C	C
Opuntia basilaris	beavertail cactus	C	C
Opuntia fulgida	jumping cactus	C	C
Opuntia leptocaulis	desert Christmas cactus	C	C
Opuntia phaeacantha	prickly pear cactus	C	S C
Opuntia polyacantha	plains prickly pear	C	S
Opuntia spinosior	cane cholla	C	C
Oryzopsis hymenoides	Indian ricegrass	G	S
Peniocereus greggii	night-blooming cereus	C	C
Phacelia spp.	phacelias	W	S C
Phlox hoodii	hood phlox	W	S
Poa fendleriana	muttongrass	G	S
Poa nevadensis	Nevada bluegrass	G	S
Poa sandbergii	secunda bluegrass	G	S
Prosopis pubescens	velvet mesquite	T	C
Prunus spp.	cherries, peaches, plums	T S	S
Purshia tridentata	antelope bitterbush	S	S
Rafinesquia neomexicana	desert chicory	W	C
Ribes spp.	currants	S	S
Rosa woodsii	Wood's rose	S	S
Sarcobatus vermiculatus	greasewood	S	S
Solidago spp.	goldenrods	W	S
Sporobolus airoides	alkali sacaton	G	S
Stipa spp.	needlegrasses	G	S
Symphoricarpos spp.	snowberries	S	S
Tetradymia glabrata	littleleaf horsebush	S	S
Yucca spp.	yuccas	C	C

offered by plants, more than 70 percent of all desert wildlife burrows underground to escape the heat. This is easily understood when you consider that just 20 inches below the surface of the soil temperatures vary only by single digits year-round.

Provide plenty of easy-burrowing space with depths of at least 20 inches and you will soon establish a wide variety of resident wildlife in your backyard habitat. Further shade the burrowing areas with plants and you'll increase their use. Even with this dependence on underground protection, desert wildlife will gather in the heaviest concentrations in those spots that offer the thickest vegetation that is also multi-storied. View your backyard as a lush, water-soaked oasis.

In the cactus desert of the Southwest, one of the most important wildlife plants is the saguaro cactus (Cereus giganteus). It provides flowers and fruits that are a feast to a wide variety of wildlife. Birds and small mammals nest in holes in its trunk, holes that are used again and again from year to year. Insects, spiders, and reptiles find an entire environment in its folds.

If your backyard borders on a wash (dry streambed), consider yourself blessed. These areas usually are the primary wildlife travel routes through the desert. Incorporate the wash into your backyard habitat by providing easy access to your oasis through a well-sheltered corridor or edge of plant life.

ROCK PILES, BRUSH PILES, AND STONE WALLS

ROCK PILES AND THEIR MORE transient counterparts – brush piles – are often best built in an inconspicuous corner of the backyard. While they are a magnet for an incredible array of shelter-seeking creatures, they often give the appearance of something left unfinished to those of the mani-cured-lawn persuasion.

Vines such as Virginia creeper or wild grape can be planted to grow over the pile, making it more aesthetic to the "civilized" eye. Unlike many actions that community standards might dictate, such planting will actually make the pile more attractive to wildlife. And, if careful choices are made, the fruits and berries of the vines will provide bountiful wildlife food.

Stone walls generally do not draw public ire like rock piles or brush piles, but they do carry similar wildlife appeal. Any child can tell you of the incredible life to be found under almost any overturned rock. Most books that I've seen on the subject of building stone walls are quick to caution of the myriad rock-dwelling creatures – some big, some small, some menacing, some charming – in their sections on collecting stone for building. The same vines that will cover potentially offensive rock piles and brush piles will also enhance the wildlife value of a stone wall.

The best rock or brush piles or stone walls are those that allow gaps among their basic building elements, while remaining sturdy. These crevices are the primary attraction for wildlife. In rock and

brush piles they can be enhanced artificially to even greater effectiveness in this respect.

Before construction of the rock or brush pile proper, lay an "X" of four 5- or 6-inch-diameter plastic or concrete drain pipes on the site. The four pieces of pipe should intersect in some larger opening, such as an overturned 18-inch-diameter (or larger) bucket that has holes cut for the pipes. The holes should be U-shaped, starting and ending at the lip opening of the bucket. The pipes should extend from this larger enclosure to the intended edge of the rock or brush pile. The pile is then built over this structure, allowing the pipe openings to be exposed to allow wildlife to enter, but camouflaged by the rocks or brush.

ABOVE: Vines can serve the dual purposes of screening some of your habitat features, such as brush and rock piles that might displease your neighbors, and providing nooks and crannies for shelter. Many species, such as wild grape (*Vitis* spp.), also set out a crop of fruit or berries that wildlife finds attractive.

It is important that the entrances/exits number at least two – even better, four – to enable the creature seeking shelter there easy escape from would-be predators. It's equally important that the entrances/exits do not slant down into the sanctuary and act as drains, as this arrangement could lead to drowning babies that are born there.

Wood piles, ABOVE, rock piles, RIGHT, and brush piles provide valuable shelter for many wildlife species, some of which won't frequent your backyard habitat without them. The key to making the piles as attractive as possible to the critters is in leaving different sized spaces between and among the various components.

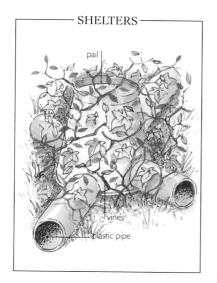

SHELTERS

pail

vines

plastic pipe

ABOVE: Many small critters, from chipmunks to toads, will make use of simple ground shelters, such as this overturned pail equipped with plastic-pipe entrances and concealed in a tangle of vines. Anchor in place.

PACIFIC COAST GARDEN

American goldfinch

MERYL FAULKNER (ABOVE) STRUGGLES WITH A UNIQUE ENVIRONMENT TO MAINTAIN AND EXPAND HER BACKYARD HABITAT IN SAN DIEGO, CALIFORNIA. LOCATED ABOUT A MILE INLAND FROM THE OCEAN AND UP ON A HILL, THE SETTING IS QUITE DRY. IN ADDITION TO ITS DRYNESS, THE SPOT REMAINS TOO WARM THROUGHOUT THE YEAR TO PROVIDE SUFFICIENT WINTER CHILLING FOR FRUIT TREES LIKE APPLE AND CHERRY TO SET THEIR FRUIT.

Dealing with this peculiar set of circumstances was one of the reasons why Faulkner got started in developing her habitat. "I didn't want to be using a lot of water," she explains, "and I wanted something that would require less maintenance than the existing lawn."

Although much of Meryl Faulkner's efforts have been directed at finding plants that would survive on her property, in the process she has provided a great deal of wildlife food, such as the scarlet sage that's attracted a nectar-gathering bumblebee, TOP LEFT, and varied bird feeders like the one that's captured the attention of a scrub jay, BELOW LEFT.

She also wanted to concentrate on plants native to her locale, both for her own enjoyment and to serve the needs of wildlife. Many of these plants have flowered so successfully that Faulkner no longer needs to maintain special hummingbird feeders.

She has also noticed that providing a complete habitat rather than just bird feeders has changed the birds' use of her property. "When we had just a lawn the birds would come to the feeder, but you wouldn't see them active on the ground," she explains.

For those backyard wildlife gardeners who want to experience the satisfaction of attracting native species, Faulkner suggests joining the nearest native plant society. A knowledgeable nursery operator with an interest in native plants can also be a tremendous help.

In the past Faulkner maintained a small ceramic bird bath, but discontinued its use after several finches drowned. Instead, she has pressed the 6-foot-diameter jacuzzi adjacent to her swimming pool into service as a makeshift bath and watering device. A blue, bubbled, plastic pool-covering material laid over the jacuzzi creates a series of shallow pools of water for birds to bathe in and drink from. In addition, the floating edges thwart any predators.

Raccoons, however, are still attracted to the swimming pool, where Faulkner houses injured seabirds she is rehabilitating. The raccoons seem less interested in the birds than in taking a dip and in

eating the fish scraps and dry cat food that the seabirds are fed.

Although her neighbors don't maintain their own wildlife habitats in their backyards, Faulkner describes them as generally supportive. One, who grows fruit for his own use, didn't even mind when gray foxes helped themselves to some of the harvest! About the biggest problem to come up has been an attack by scrub jays on one neighbor's vinyl lawn chair to steal some of the stuffing. Another problem was caused by a skunk digging up a nearby lawn whose owners took great pains to maintain in perfect condition. This was quickly solved with a live trap.

Faulkner advises new backyard habitatters, "If you want to attract wildlife, first check whether you're going to have a problem with domestic animals (primarily cats). If you do, hang the feeders where the cats will have difficulty getting to them – don't set your birds up for some domestic cat from two houses up."

When local cats began preying on her songbird population, she tried to thwart them with a small electrified fence. But that idea was scrapped as soon as a towhee was zapped. Then she hung her feeders out over a 15-foot slope; since

then she has had no problems.

Birds of prey will take advantage of the concentrations of smaller birds that well-managed backyard habitats create, but Faulkner sees this as part of the natural order of things. "You must allow for the fact that you're going to have a Cooper's hawk come through and take a dove or a sparrow every now and then."

Some of the wildlife-attracting plants in the Faulkner habitat:

beach evening primrose, beach sagebrush, blue flax, bottlebrush, buckwheats, buddleia, California fan palm, California fuchsia, California tree mallow, carpenteria, coral bells, golden currant, groundcover rosemary, island snapdragon, lemon tree, monkey flower, native sage, penstemons, pyracantha, quail bush, St. Catherine's lace, spicebush, strawberry tree, summer holly, wallflower, woolly blue curls

Some of the wildlife sighted in the Faulkner habitat:

BIRDS
American goldfinch, Anna's hummingbird, brown towhee, bushtit, California quail, Costa's hummingbird, field sparrow, hawk (various species), house finch, junco, mockingbird, mourning dove, northern flicker, orange-crowned warbler, roadrunner, scrub jay, western tanager, white-crowned sparrow, Wilson's warbler

MAMMALS
California ground squirrel, coyote, gray fox, opossum, raccoon, skunk

Many plants attractive to wildlife species also provide wonderful color that would be welcome in any backyard, such as this yarrow, TOP RIGHT, and bottlebrush, RIGHT.

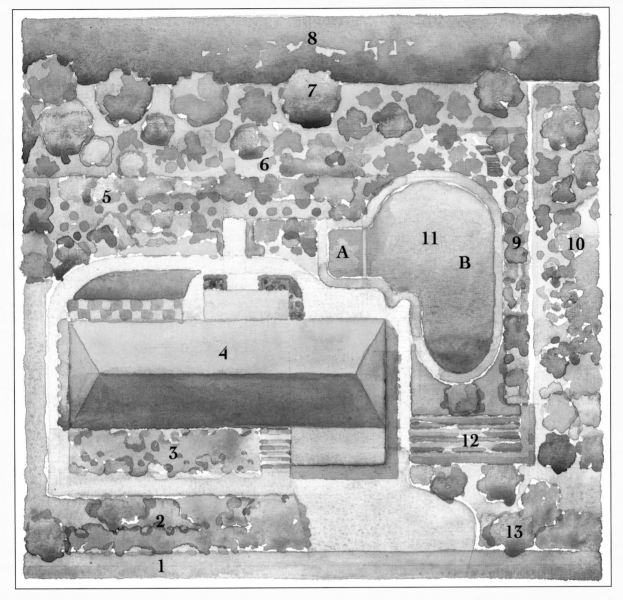

FAULKNER HABITAT

1 street
2 pyracantha, bottlebrush, roses, torrey pine
3 roses
4 house with patio and balcony
5 stepping stones; mixed flowers
6 downward sloping bank planted with baccharis, wild buckwheat, artemisia, and rosemary

7 pines, eucalyptus
8 fence with canyon beyond
9 perennials with chain-link fence in back
10 bank planted with ground cover, mixed shrubs, and trees; bordering canyon
11 pool and jacuzzi
12 vegetables
13 plum, mulberry, cedar, ceanothus

A water for drinking and bathing
B refuge for injured seabirds

A FULLY FUNCTIONING NATURAL ECOSYSTEM

When all of these habitat elements – at least all of those that naturally occur within a given region – have been assembled and the wildlife has moved in, we have what is known as an ecosystem. A fully functioning natural ecosystem includes all the associated wildlife, plants, water, soil and other earth features, and atmosphere.

Most often the average backyard habitatter creates a partial ecosystem. The size limitations of the property that most of us have to work with simply cannot provide an entire ecosystem. We may provide everything that some creatures need to live their entire lives within the confines of our habitat, but others that naturally interact with those creatures may need more space or may be reluctant to come into close contact with humans. They sometimes frequent our habitat.

This need not be too much of a concern for us. If we do everything that we can to provide all the elements of the habitats outlined throughout this book, wildlife will benefit and be attracted into our backyards. Nevertheless, the concept of ecosystem helps us to understand why many of our wildlife guests are not present at the time.

SUCCESSION

Another concept that the backyard habitatter should understand is succession. This is the gradual and natural change over time from one type of habitat to another.

In the wild state, succession might transform a site from the bare ground that was the bottom of a pond into a field of wildflowers, into a mixture of these plants and low shrubs, into a blend of larger shrubs, small trees, and wildflowers that can tolerate shade, then into a forest.

The forest stage, known as the climax stage in this example, is the most stable of the habitat types and may last for many decades as a self-maintaining community. However, eventually something, like fire or human action, may destroy the forest and begin the succession process anew.

In the backyard, succession means that the habitat elements that you design and plant and nurture along will change. For example, if left to natural forces, the thicket of shrubs, briars, wildflowers, and weeds that you created would eventually become a small

SUCCESSION AND EDGE

bare field

grasses and wildflowers

shrubs

edge

small trees

edge

climax forest

ABOVE: The gradual change of habitat from one type to another is known as succession. Any point where two different environments come together is known as edge. Edge holds some elements from each environment and is highly attractive to nearly all wildlife.

LEFT and RIGHT: The elements of succession, which is the gradual change over time from one type of habitat to another through natural processes, can be built into any backyard habitat with some planning for the future. A simple way to understand this concept and incorporate it into your plan is to re-visit a wooded area that you've been familiar with for many years. Try to remember as many specific details from before and compare them to what exists in the same spot now. If you have some old photos of the spot, take them along for direct comparison.

wood lot. This will take many years to occur and intervention by you at any point along the way can alter the process.

As the plant community changes, so does the wildlife. Some of the species that thrived in the thicket habitat may not be able to find the shelter and food they need in the wood lot. On the small scale of a backyard habitat, the wildlife will simply move to a more appropriate habitat.

MAINTENANCE AND PEST CONTROL

AS YOU ATTRACT WILDLIFE into your backyard, many species will be harmless or even beneficial. But they will be accompanied by pest species as well, and the most noticeable among these will be the insects that attack your garden.

Nature's solution is a teeter-totter balance between harmful species, species that prey upon them, and natural repellent reactions in plants. That is certainly one approach, but it's not one that will leave much for you in your vegetable garden or on your fruit trees.

The garden industry can offer a veritable toxic waste dump of chemical solutions. But these are counterproductive and even destructive to everything you're trying to achieve with a backyard habitat.

Luckily, public sentiment has been swinging in favor of organic, natural methods of pest control for several years. An arsenal of these environmentally safer measures is now available.

One of the most highly publicized, most enjoyable, and environmentally sound methods of pest control in the backyard habitat is the introduction of beneficial insects. However, while these insects do destroy many harmful pests, there continues to be much debate over just how effective they may be against any particular pest species and over the gardener's ability to restrict them to the desired location.

Many of these desirable species, such as praying mantises, ladybugs, and lacewings, have disappeared from many backyards and gardens as the owners came to rely more and more on chemical pesticides. The poisons may have done away with the targeted problem species temporarily, but in many cases, they permanently removed these beneficial species as well.

Now, the trend is in the opposite direction. Each year more garden supply companies offer an increasingly diverse list of beneficial insects for home use. They will destroy an incredible number of pest species, but their even greater allure may be the special charm they bring to our backyards. For many of us, the strange posture of the praying mantis and the swarming color of ladybugs are fond childhood memories that somehow got lost along the way.

Birds, toads, and frogs are likewise effective pest control measures that many pesticide advocates seem to shun from their tightly controlled backyards. There are simple measures available to attract all of them into the backyard, which will be explained in subsequent chapters.

The home garden industry has also come up with a large arsenal of homemade and organic defenses against pest species. Many of these are detailed in the accompanying table on page 77.

And, for those who can't wean themselves completely from the use of something commercially available in a can or jar, or who have severe infestations that natural methods simply cannot handle, there are many organic pesticides derived from plants.

These include: rotenone, an extract of tropical plants; pyrethrum, derivative of the pyrethrum flower, *Chrysanthemum cinerariifolium*; sabadilla, from the plant *Schoenocaulon officinalis*; and ryania, made from ground roots of the shrub *Ryania speciosa*. Many commercially available organic solutions contain combinations of these.

While these are organic, they are still very strong pesticides and will kill many beneficial species as well as the targeted pests. Consider them your last alternative in reaction to an infestation rather than as a preventive measure.

For many insect pests in small garden or home situations, the simplest approach is often quite effective. Physically pick the pests from your plants. Determining favorite hiding places and removing these, or using them as daily traps for physical picking, is also effective against many species. Removal of all garden rubbish each fall is a strong preventive measure. And, planting resistant vegetable cultivars will head off many problems.

BIRDS AND MAMMALS THAT HELP THEMSELVES

Insects are not your only potential problems in the vegetable garden. Many species of birds and mammals also are eager to help themselves to your crops.

But, in this respect, developing a backyard habitat often proves to be part of the solution rather than

LEFT: Even as they emerge from their egg cases, young praying mantises are looking for their first meal. If nothing else is handy, they'll set upon each other.

PERSISTENT PROBLEMS

electrified wire to discourage raccoons

wire below ground to discourage digging

ABOVE: The groundhog is probably the most tenacious of backyard pests. Keeping the animal out of the vegetable or flower garden requires fencing that extends both above and below ground level.

RIGHT and FAR RIGHT: Many bird species are highly effective predator controls on the local insect populations. Some, like this eastern bluebird, require a high proportion of insects in their diet year-round. Others are more inclined toward insect prey when feeding nests of young. Of course, a habitat completely "cleansed" of all its insects would lack such interesting features as this maple leaf gall.

the problem. More than a few backyard habitatters have discovered the preference of most birds for wild berries over cultivated fruits. Others would quickly argue the point.

Garden netting generally is quite effective against bird raids on your berry bushes and dwarf fruit trees. A full 100 percent effectiveness is not to be expected, however. Nearly everyone with these plants has a story or two about the birds that got under the netting.

For lower-lying plants, such as strawberries and sprouting vegetables, portable cages also will give good protection against birds and small mammals, such as chipmunks. Thread strung between stakes in a criss-cross pattern over the young plants is another bird preventive.

Groundhogs, also known as woodchucks, are the most persistent of mammal marauders. Nearly every home remedy, short of adequate fencing, ever tried against them has come up short. In groundhog terms, adequate fencing means garden fencing that extends at least 12 inches below the surface of the ground and several feet above the surface. Angling the below-ground portion of the fence outward from the garden at 90 degrees for a few feet also has been known to thwart these quite able diggers. This same fencing, if the space between wires is small enough, will also keep rabbits, skunks, opossums, and similar animals out of the garden.

Larger species, such as the white-tailed deer, will simply step

or jump over any fence that stands less than 8 feet in height. Chicken wire laid flat on the ground around the perimeter of the garden at a width of 3 or 4 feet, however, will thwart most of their efforts.

Raccoons are another special case. Only two types of fencing are effective against them: fencing that includes a complete roof of fence over the fenced-in area and fencing topped with a strand or two of electrified wire along the top. Both of these have major drawbacks. The first is expensive, labor-intensive, and potentially disturbing to neighbors. The second is prohibited in many municipalities and deserves deep consideration before installing in any residential area.

BELOW: Woodchucks are among the most persistent of pests in the backyard, particularly a backyard with a vegetable garden. Strong fencing, extending below ground, is essential.

ABOVE: Lady beetles are very beneficial predators in the backyard habitat, feeding on such destructive pest species as aphids.

LEFT: Most wildlife species bring both positive and negative aspects with them, although to most backyard habitatters the positive generally outweighs the negative. For example, the caterpillar of the palmedes swallowtail butterfly eventually becomes a magnificent butterfly, but it first devours a considerable amount of foliage, possibly including some of your favorite ornamentals. Similarly, the field mouse is a cute and adorable guest in your backyard habitat. It can also be very destructive when it begins searching for comfortable nesting quarters, which might just be inside the walls of your home. Each habitatter must make his or her own peace with this inherent conflict, deciding just how much damage is acceptable given the special characteristics that a species brings with it. Of course, it is possible to maintain some buffering distance by careful placement of wildlife-attracting features.

Natural Methods of Control

PEST	NATURAL CONTROL
Ants	Lay a border of steamed bonemeal or powdered charcoal to keep out of garden; band plants and tree trunks to prevent climbing; pour scalding water into nests.
Aphids	Ladybugs; onion, garlic, hot pepper, or lime (mixed with water) sprays; spray of soapy water left on infected plants for several hours and then washed off; trap in a pan painted bright yellow and filled with soapy water.
Bean beetles	Praying mantises; interplant beans with potatoes, nasturtiums, or garlic.
Cabbage maggots	Four parts wood ashes to one part each lime, rock phosphate, and bonemeal applied to soil in 2-foot radius around each cabbage.
Cabbageworms	Interplant cabbage with onion, garlic, sage, rosemary, and hyssop; apply Bt (*Bacillus thuringiensis*).
Codling moths	Trichogramma wasps; woodpeckers; wrap corrugated paper or burlap around trunks of fruit trees about five weeks after petal fall, remove and burn after moth larvae have spun cocoons in them.
Corn borers	Ladybugs; trichogramma wasps; plant corn after egg-laying in early season; resistant corn cultivars.
Corn earworms	Trichogramma wasps; Bt (*Bacillus thuringiensis*); apply half a medicine dropper of mineral oil to corn silk when begins to turn brown.
Cucumber beetles	For small crop, cover plants with cheesecloth as soon as they are up (keep edges of cheesecloth in contact with soil); interplant with radishes, marigolds, and nasturtiums; spraying with rotenone may be needed for heavy infestations.
Cutworms	Remove all mulch and weeds each fall as a preventive measure; 3-inch-wide collar around each young plant; interplant with onions; crushed eggshells, wood ashes, or builder's sand at base of plants.
Earwigs	Trap in newspapers, old carpeting, or folded black plastic in shady areas; shake daily into bucket of water and few drops kerosene.
Japanese beetles	Commercially available traps; milky spore disease.
Mealybugs	*Cryptolaemus montrouzieri* (beetles); lacewings; soapy water spray.
Mosquitoes	Purple martins; dragonflies; toads; frogs; praying mantises; spread thin oil film over stagnant water before egg-hatching time; sassafras and castor oil plants (*Ricinus* spp.)
Nematodes	Removal of all plants (garden and weed) from infected area for three or four years, burning roots of all infected plants.
Leafhoppers	Interplant with petunias or geraniums (*Pelargonium* spp.); diatomaceous earth around plants.
Peach borers	Wrap fruit tree trunks with cotton batting and cover that with black plastic; cultivate around base of fruit trees frequently in spring; apply tanglefoot from 1 inch below soil to 1 foot above; plant garlic around tree base; sprinkle 2-inch-wide ring of tobacco dust around base.
Roaches	Garlic cloves as repellent; pine oil sprayed where roaches are found.
Scales	Ladybugs; spray fruit trees with dormant oil in late winter; soapy water spray.
Slugs and snails	Oak leaf mulch as repellent; beer or teaspoon of baking yeast to 3 ounces of water in low saucer; border of ashes, cinders, sand, or diatomaceous earth; corrugated aluminum edging; spray of wormwood (*Artemisia absinthium*) tea.
Sow bugs and pill bugs	Eliminate hiding places such as boards and stones near garden; onion-water spray.
Spider mites	Ladybugs; onion, garlic, or chive spray; treat fruit trees with dormant oil in late winter.
Squash borers	Interplant with radishes, nasturtiums, marigolds, and tansy; severe infestations may require spraying with rotenone, but only after all ripe squash have been removed.
Tent caterpillars	Praying mantises; wearing gloves, remove "tents" from trees and step on all the worms; burlap around tree trunks will trap mature larvae for daily collection.
Tomato hornworms	Praying mantises; trichogramma wasps; interplant with borage, basil, and marigolds; Bt (*Bacillus thuringiensis*).

INSECTS – YOUR FIRST VISITORS

DESPITE ANY RELUCTANCE on your part, insects and spiders will be the most immediate immigrants into the backyard habitat that you've created with your plants. After all, there are more insects and spiders – both in sheer numbers and in numbers of species – than any other group of animals. More than 100,000 species have been identified in North America. In addition, the world for most of these creatures is tiny by comparison to most other forms of animal life. A backyard is like a universe to many of them.

To get the fullest enjoyment out of all possible aspects of the backyard habitat you've created, old preconceptions about insects and spiders are best discarded right now. These creatures are going to be very much a part of your experience in this environment. If you are open to the additional worlds of discovery that they offer, you will find the overall experience much less stressful and more satisfying.

Many of the insect and spider species, of course, will have been residents of your property for many years before you did anything special to attract them. You've struggled with their ancestors, probably since you bought the property. But with luck, you are now looking at them as though for the first time, through a new perspective.

The real pest species that you've been contending with in the vegetable and flower gardens all along are still there. And rest assured that the development of a better habitat

ABOVE: There'll be much more life in a backyard habitat than the highly visible birds and "cuddly" mammals. An almost invisible world, including creatures such as this banded garden spider, is waiting to reveal itself on close, hands-and-knees investigation.

will definitely bring some new ones on the run.

With them, however, you may now notice some welcome species as the result of all your efforts as a habitatter. Butterflies are the group that comes immediately to mind as relatively harmless and enjoyable. As the native plants that you've added to the community in your

backyard begin to blossom, these delights of flitting color will appear.

RELAX AND ENJOY YOUR HABITAT

The most effective thing you can do at this point to encourage as many different insect species as possible is sit back and enjoy the passing spectacle of life. The less you do with the backyard habitat, once the plant communities are established for the year, the better most insects and spiders will like it.

The two things that most people do with their backyards – applying herbicides, fungicides, and pesticides, and mowing – literally spell death for the insects and spiders.

Even those garden sprays and solutions not intended to kill them often do just that. Mowing maintains grasses and other plants at levels where relatively few species can make much use of them.

This is not to say that you should sell the lawn mower. As we said before, this is still your backyard. Maintain as much of it as you want in manicured lawn and give the rest to wildlife.

If "the rest" can include an unmowed section at the back fence or in some other out-of-the-way place, the insects will thrive there – especially if wildflowers and other native plants are encouraged to fill the space.

The lawn areas that might be adjacent to these wild sections still are welcomed by the insects. Being cold-blooded, many of them are most active in sun-filled areas where their body temperatures can benefit from the solar radiation. Some will spend nearly their entire lives in those open areas, but a great many more will find the food and shelter they need in the "weed patch."

As you have undoubtedly relearned many times in moving rocks, logs, debris, and the like around the backyard, many species of insects are attracted to the undersides of these objects. As we've discussed previously, a fallen log is a great attractant of myriad life. Stone and brush piles will also serve as magnets.

To enjoy the greatest diversity of insect and spider life in the areas where you want them, posi-

tion such hiding places directly in and near the wild-plant plots. Add a small, very shallow ($\frac{1}{4}$–$\frac{1}{2}$ inch) water source and you'll be amazed at the number of species that make their homes there.

Even on a tiny lot in our largest cities the potential result of such effort is mind-boggling. More than 15,000 insect and spider species have been documented in New York City, for example.

UNDERSTANDING THE INSECT LIFE

Insects pass through several stages of life en route from egg to adult. Some, such as grasshoppers, emerge from the egg as miniature replicas of their adult selves. They simply pass through a number of stages of growth and molting (skin shedding) to become

adults. This is known as simple metamorphosis.

Others, such as cicadas, pass through several nymph stages growing and developing wings, before becoming adults. This is incomplete metamorphosis.

And many, including butterflies and moths, hatch from the egg as a larva (a caterpillar for butterflies and moths), which feeds and then enters the resting pupa (cocoon) stage. The adult emerges from the pupa. This is complete metamorphosis.

BELOW: Many of the lower forms of life, such as insects, pass through various stages before becoming adults. Shown here is the butterfly cycle, from egg through caterpillar and chrysalis to adult.

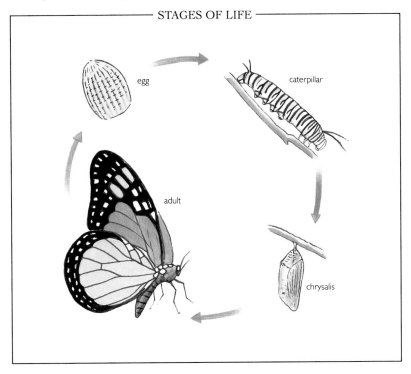

STAGES OF LIFE

egg

caterpillar

adult

chrysalis

BUTTERFLIES AND MOTHS

ALL THE SPECIAL MEASURES required to attract other insects apply equally to efforts to bring butterflies and moths into the backyard.

BUTTERFLIES IN PARTICULAR

Flowers are even more crucial to success with butterflies than with many other insect species. But, from the butterfly's perspective, flowers are much more than the domestic ornamentals that the word conjures for many humans. Even some of our more noxious weeds provide for the needs of many butterfly species.

The much scorned dandelion is a nectar source for species including the cabbage white, comma, common sulphur, red admiral, and sara orangetip. The invasive milkweed serves as the primary food source for the caterpillars of the monarch and queen and a nectar source for very many butterflies, including the American painted lady, cabbage white, checkered white, common blue, common sulphur, eastern black swallowtail, giant swallowtail, gray hairstreak, fiery skipper, great spangled fritillary, hackberry butterfly, monarch, mourning cloak, orange sulphur, painted lady, pearly crescentspot, pipevine swallowtail, queen, question mark, red admiral, spicebush swallowtail, spring azure, tiger swallowtial, viceroy, and western tiger swallowtail.

Nettles attract the question mark, comma, satyr anglewing and Milbert's tortoiseshell.

Plants to Attract Butterflies and Moths

BOTANICAL NAME	COMMON NAME	BUTTERFLY
Althaea spp.	hollyhocks	common checkered skipper, painted lady
Amorpha spp.	false indigos	dogface butterfly, marine blue
Anaphalis spp.	everlastings	American painted lady, painted lady
Antennaria spp.	pussy-toes	American painted lady, painted lady
Antirrhinum spp.	snapdragons	buckeye
Apocynum spp.	dogbanes	American painted lady, buckeye, checkered white, common sulphur, gray hairstreak, mourning cloak, orange sulphur, pearly crescentspot, silver-spotted skipper, spicebush swallowtail, spring azure, tawny-edged skipper
Arabis spp.	rock cresses	falcate orangetip, Milbert's tortoiseshell, mourning cloak, sara orangetip, spring azure
Arctium spp.	burdocks	American painted lady, painted lady
Aristolochia spp.	pipevines	pipevine swallowtail
Artemisia spp.	artemisias	American painted lady, buckeye, painted lady
Asclepias spp.	milkweeds	American painted lady, cabbage white, checkered white, common blue, common sulphur, eastern black swallowtail, fiery skipper, gaint swallowtail, gray hairstreak, great spangled fritillary, hackberry butterfly, monarch, mourning cloak, orange sulphur, painted lady, pearly crescentspot, pipevine swallowtail, queen, question mark, red admiral, spicebush swallowtail, spring azure, tiger swallowtail, viceroy
Aster spp.	asters	American painted lady, buckeye, checkered white, common checkered skipper, common sulphur, fiery skipper, Milbert's tortoiseshell, orange sulphur, painted lady, pearly crescentspot, question mark, red admiral
Atriplex spp.	salt bushes	eastern pygmy blue
Aureolaria pedicularia	false foxglove	buckeye
Baptisia spp.	baptisias	American painted lady, buckeye, painted lady
Barbarea spp.	winter cresses	brown elfin, cabbage white, checkered white, falcate orangetip, gray hairstreak, pearly crescentspot, silver-spotted skipper
Bidens spp.	beggar-ticks	common checkered skipper, fiery skipper, gulf fritillary, monarch, queen, red admiral, viceroy
Buddleia spp.	butterfly bushes	American painted lady, anise swallowtail, comma, Milbert's tortoiseshell, mourning cloak, painted lady, pipevine swallowtail, red admiral, tiger swallowtail
Celtis spp.	hackberries	hackberry butterfly, mourning cloak, question mark
Centaurea spp.	knapweeds	American painted lady, common checkered skipper, common sulphur, fiery skipper

BOTANICAL NAME	COMMON NAME	BUTTERFLY
Cephalanthus spp.	buttonbushes	American painted lady, monarch, painted lady, tiger swallowtail
Chenopodium spp.	lamb's quarters	American painted lady, buckeye, painted lady
Chrysanthemum spp.	chrysanthemums, daisies	cloudless giant sulphur, fiery skipper, Milbert's tortoiseshell, pearly crescentspot, queen, red admiral
Chrysothamnus nauseosus	gray rabbitbush	orange sulphur, painted lady
Cichorium intybus	common chicory	buckeye
Cirsium spp.	thistles	American painted lady, dogface butterfly, gulf fritillary, Milbert's tortoiseshell, monarch, painted lady, pearly crescentspot, pipevine swallowtail, silver-spotted skipper, spicebush swallowtail, red admiral, tawny-edged skipper, tiger swallowtail, viceroy, western tiger swallowtail
Clethra alnifolia	sweet pepperbush	American painted lady, question mark, red admiral, red-spotted purple, spicebush swallowtail
Coreopsis grandiflora	tickseed	buckeye, common sulphur, monarch, orange sulphur, pearly crescentspot
Daucus carota subsp. *carota*		Queen-Anne's-lace eastern black swallowtail, gray hairstreak
Daucus carota var. *sativus*	carrot	anise swallowtail, eastern black swallowtail
Echinacea spp.	purple coneflowers	great spangled fritillary, silvery blue, tawny-edged skipper
Epilobium spp.	fireweeds	red admiral
Gaylussacia spp.	huckleberries	brown elfin
Gnaphalium spp.	everlastings	American painted lady, painted lady
Gramineae	grass family	fiery skipper, large wood nymph, tawny-edged skipper
Humulus spp.	hops	comma, question mark, red admiral
Lantana spp.	lantanas	anise swallowtail, cabbage white, fiery skipper, gulf fritillary, spicebush swallowtail
Laportea canadensis	wood nettle	comma, red admiral
Lathyrus odoratus	sweet pea	gray hairstreak, marine blue, silvery blue
Ligustrum spp.	privets	American painted lady, painted lady, red-spotted purple, silver-spotted skipper, spring azure
Lindera benzoin	spicebush	spicebush swallowtail
Lupinus spp.	lupines	common blue, silvery blue
Malus spp.	apples	red-spotted purple, spring azure, viceroy
Malva spp.	mallows	American painted lady, gray hairstreak, monarch, painted lady, red admiral
Medicago sativa	alfalfa	dogface butterfly, eastern black swallowtail, large wood nymph, orange sulphur, tawny-edged skipper
Mentha x piperita	peppermint	pearly crescentspot
Mentha spp.	mints	American painted lady, anise swallowtail, cabbage white, gray hairstreak, large wood nymph, monarch, red admiral, western black swallowtail, western tiger swallowtail

(continued)

SPECIAL EFFORTS FOR MOTHS

The most beneficial thing you can do for moths and night-flying insects is to disconnect your back-yard bug zappers. These are indiscriminate killers, and there is some informal evidence that they kill many more harmless species than those pest species for which they are intended.

You might be surprised at just how many different types of night-fliers your backyard actually attracts. There are two very simple methods for gaining some insight in this area.

ABOVE: Even a single window box can be a habitat of sorts. Fully planted, like this one, a box of flowers can attract many insects species, as well as some birds and small mammals.

Hang an old white sheet between two trees or over a fence and shine a bright light onto it. Just as they do at street and porch lights, the moths will gather at the light and settle on the sheet.

A technique known as sugaring also will bring moths into easy-viewing situations. It can be used in the same manner that seeds are placed in feeders for birds.

Make a bait by blending brown sugar (melted over a low heat), stale beer, and rotten fruit (bananas and peaches work best) into a pulp that will adhere to woody surfaces. Recipes vary about the exact quantities of each ingredient, but many call for about a four-to-one ratio of sugar to beer and enough fruit to make the concoction fragrant.

Tree trunks at various locations throughout the backyard make optimum "feeders." But logs, wooden fence posts, and the like will serve just as well. The mixture should be spread thickly by paintbrush on these surfaces at dusk. You can also soak cloth strips in the mixture and suspend them from branches. If you intend to view the moths later, it is a good idea to place the bait about chest high, which allows for easier viewing.

Wait until after dark and then approach the baited locations slowly. Your light should not be shone directly on the bait. Shine the beam first on the ground at the base of the baited surface. Some moth species will react to the light by dropping to the ground, disturbing any that might be resting or feeding below them.

BOTANICAL NAME	COMMON NAME	BUTTERFLY
Petroselinum crispum	parsley	anise swallowtail, eastern black swallowtail
Populus spp.	aspens, poplars	mourning cloak, red-spotted purple, viceroy, western tiger swallowtail, white admiral
Prunus spp.	cherries, peaches, plums	red-spotted purple, spring azure, viceroy
Rudbeckia hirta	black-eyed Susan	great spangled fritillary, pearly crescentspot
Salix spp.	willows	brown elfin, mourning cloak, red-spotted purple, tiger swallowtail, western tiger swallowtail, white admiral
Scabiosa spp.	scabiosas	American painted lady, painted lady
Sedum spp.	stonecrops	Milbert's tortoiseshell, painted lady, red admiral
Solidago spp.	goldenrods	American painted lady, common sulphur, gray hairstreak, Milbert's tortoiseshell, orange sulphur, red admiral, viceroy
Tagetes spp.	marigolds	American painted lady, Milbert's tortoiseshell
Taraxacum spp.	dandelions	cabbage white, comma, common sulphur, red admiral, sara orangetip
Trifolium pratense	red clover	American painted lady, cabbage white, common checkered skipper, great spangled fritillary, painted lady, red admiral, silver spotted skipper, tawny-edged skipper
Ulmus spp.	elms	comma, mourning cloak
Urtica spp.	nettles	comma, Milbert's tortoiseshell, question mark, satyr anglewing
Vaccinium spp.	blueberries	brown elfin
Verbena spp.	verbenas	buckeye, great spangled fritillary
Vernonia spp.	ironweeds	American painted lady, fiery skipper, great spangled fritillary, monarch, tiger swallowtail
Vicia spp.	vetches	American painted lady, common sulphur, gray hairstreak, orange sulphur, silvery blue
Viola spp.	violets	great spangled fritillary, spring azure

RIGHT: An incredible array of moths and other flying insects probably frequent your backyard each night without your ever noticing. A white sheet suspended as shown here, or hung over a laundry line, with a lamp or flashlight behind it, will draw them in for close observation.

NIGHT PATROL

CONSIDERATIONS FOR AMPHIBIANS AND REPTILES

AMPHIBIANS AND REPTILES, being small, relatively slow-moving, and highly environment-dependent creatures, have been particularly hard-hit by the changes that people have brought to the world. It's amazing that any have been able to survive in our developed areas.

Many amphibians pass through annual migrations to and from water for purposes of courting, mating, and laying eggs. Although some of these migratory movements may be small, in developed areas they are generally enough to expose the creatures to danger from people, their pets, and the tires of their machines. Even for those amphibians that successfully complete the migrations, the water sources available to them may be too contaminated for the resulting eggs to produce a new generation.

Reptiles tend to lay large, shelled eggs that they must bury for concealment and protection. Very little of the land developed by people offers much in the way of suitable habitats.

But a few of these animals, like the amphibious bullfrog, even seem to be thriving. Drainage ditches, depressions on vacant lots, and ponds in city parks provide ample testament to this.

Much of what we've discussed earlier will reverse these negative conditions, at least on your property, transforming segments of your habitat into prime amphibian and reptile space.

An in-ground water source, kept filled with clean water, will do more for many amphibian species than anything else you can do in the backyard. Their use of the area will be further enhanced if the water source is bordered on at least two sides with thick native grasses and wetland plants over moist soil. Add a few rotting logs, and you'll have a nearly irresistible environment for whatever amphibians still may live in your area.

Drier areas with rock piles or stone walls and sandy, easy-digging soils will serve the reptiles. A portion of this area should be fully exposed to the sun to provide an essential warming area for these cold-blooded, sun-loving creatures. The rest of the area should be shaded by vegetation, because even the reptiles need to escape the sun at times.

Amphibians and reptiles will amply reward your efforts by eating thousands of harmful insects over the course of a summer. For the American toad, for example, estimates range to upward of 200 for the number of insects that one toad can eat in one night.

BELOW: Forget the myths about warts. Toads should be welcomed into the backyard habitat as relatively passive guests, although they are not all that passive toward their insect prey.

CANADIAN SOUTHEAST GARDEN

ON THE ACCOMPANYING SKETCH OF THE PROPERTY OF BOB KEIR AND JOANNA TAYLOR (ABOVE) IN SUDBURY, ONTARIO, CANADA, YOU'LL NOTICE A LOT OF ROCKS AND ROCK GROUPINGS INDICATED. LIKE MUCH OF THIS CITY, THE PROPERTY WAS CARVED FROM THE ROCKY TERRAIN OF THE PRECAMBRIAN SHIELD. AREAS OF ROCK WERE DYNAMITED AWAY FOR THE HOUSES AND THEIR BASEMENTS TO BE BUILT, AND THE PROPERTIES WERE THEN BACKFILLED.

ABOVE: Bob Keir and Joanna Taylor maintain more of their property as traditional lawn and garden than many backyard habitatters, but they have included many extras that fill the site with a wide variety of wildlife species. Their nestboxes, feeders, and cluster plantings of flowers and shrubs are very attractive, both aesthetically and to wildlife. The property also features food-producing trees, such as birch.

The couple has worked to carve out their backyard habitat within the natural constraints of the property. As much of the habitat as possible has been created with what nature has provided. All of the borders have been constructed from rocks found on the property and fallen trees that were killed by a previous forest fire.

A large granite boulder that was left on-site when the property was cleared for construction has been made into a bird bath. This is the only water source for the habitat, a situation that Keir hopes to remedy soon with the addition of a recirculating pool. Here again, he plans to

American toad

use the existing landscape by incorporating the pool at the base of a large boulder that will provide a waterfall with a drop of about 5 feet.

Although Keir's advice to new backyard habitatters is to be prepared for a lot of hard work, he sees his unique property as a site with "a lot of character" rather than a lot of obstacles. He prefers the many hills, valleys, and rock outcrops to a flat, uniform site. "We've sort of sculptured around them," he says of the features in his up-and-down terrain.

Developing his backyard is a task he never expects to complete fully. "There's always something else that can be done, adding this or adding that, or taking something out. With imagination, there's really no end to what you can do."

The couple has maintained an element of human use and human enjoyment within the habitat they've created. For example, a park bench placed at the rear of the property provides a completely different viewpoint for visitors from that on the deck at the rear of the house.

The trees that dot the landscape, with the exception of the few spruce and one red maple, were all self-sown. So Keir's primary effort has been with the swampy areas.

Soon after moving in, he had 85 yards of fill deposited on the site. That has been followed by another 30 yards in the intervening years. He also adds about 40 to 50 yards of sod per year.

However, he says if he were starting a backyard wildlife garden from scratch on a newly developed site, he would look first at the trees. If there were only a few, he would start planting more trees immediately. He would concentrate on evergreens for the shelter they provide to wildlife and place them close to where he planned to provide water and food.

In several places Keir has allowed the grass to go unmowed and grow tall. His aim is for the free-growing grasses to occupy the niche that many noxious weeds would otherwise fill. In other places around the house, beds of flowers have been planted to attract hummingbirds and butterflies.

A martin house is included among the habitat's offerings and, although scout birds do visit the backyard each spring, the property's trees have grown too large and provide too much of an overstory for the birds to set up housekeeping. However, martin houses on some other properties in the neighborhood do attract colonies of purple martins.

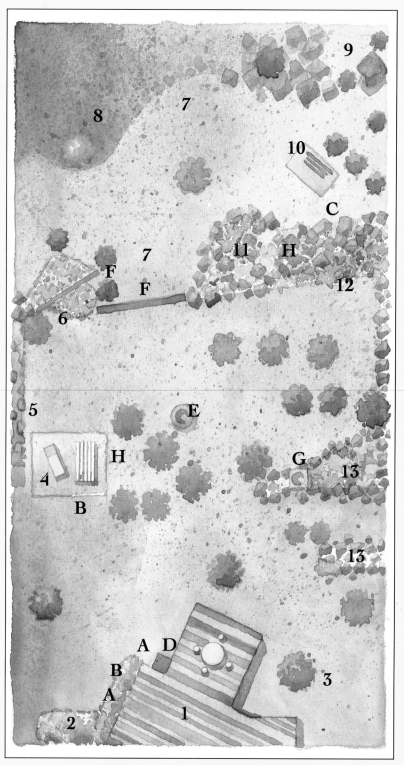

KEIR HABITAT
1 house with wood deck
2 mixed flowers
3 pansies around white birch
4 stone patio with picnic table
and bench
5 ivy-covered buildings
6 sugar maples; mixed flowers
7 grass slope
8 scrub, white birch
9 rock
10 patio stones, park bench
11 rock cluster planted with impatiens
and euonymus shrubs
12 pine root edging around sugar
maples and mixed flowers
13 rocks with mixed flowers

A feeder
B hummingbird feeder
C covered tray feeder
D composter
E bird bath
F pine log
G martin house
H electrical outlet

BELOW: Traditional backyard fixtures
like the pedestal-type birdbath, when
combined with "wilder" features like
this stand of trees and wooded hillside,
can create a parklike setting.

About a half-dozen feeders of different types are scattered about the habitat throughout much of the year. However, for ease of maintenance these are all moved closer to the house in the winter. This practice led to one of the more unusual visitors to the backyard a few years ago, when a ruffed grouse took up residence. The bird visited a tray feeder filled with sunflower seeds on the deck twice each day, just before daybreak and again at dusk. Eventually it grew tame enough not to fly off as soon as it spotted someone.

Among the other interesting happenings in the backyard was a cowbird chick being fed by its much smaller chipping sparrow foster parent. (Cowbirds are notorious for laying their eggs in the nests of other birds and leaving the hatchlings for these foster parents to raise.)

Of course, the property has its expected population of squirrels. One in particular continues to present an amusing challenge to the couple as they try to find new ways to prevent it from gaining access to their bird feeders.

Some of the wildlife-attracting plants found in the Keir habitat:

TREES
Colorado spruce, red maple, sugar maple, white birch

SHRUBS AND VINES
euonymus, juniper, lilac

FLOWERS AND HERBS
basil, bleeding heart, chives, citronella pelargonium, clematis, coleus, daffodil, dahlia, fuchsia, geranium, gladiolus, hens-and-chickens, impatiens, Johnny-jump-up, lily-of-the-valley, lobelia, marigold, nicotiana, oregano, pansy, parsley, peony, periwinkle, petunia, phlox, poppy, primrose, rose, scilla, shasta daisy, snapdragon, spike, thyme, tuberous begonia, tulip, violet, wax begonia

Some of the wildlife sighted in the Keir habitat:

BIRDS
American goldfinch, American robin, black-capped chickadee, blue jay, chipping sparrow, common crow, common grackle, European starling, evening grosbeak, house sparrow, junco, mourning dove, pine siskin, purple finch, purple martin, red-breasted nuthatch, redpoll, ruby-throated hummingbird, ruffed grouse, snow bunting, white-breasted nuthatch, white-crowned sparrow

MAMMALS
chipmunk, mole, red squirrel, striped skunk

REPTILES AND AMPHIBIANS
American toad, green frog

LEFT: The landscape plan places many of the wildlife-attracting plants close to the home, where the various species can be viewed through the windows. This method causes less disturbance to the wildlife.

BIRD FEEDERS AND SEEDS

BIRD FEEDING IS PROBABLY the image that first comes to mind for most people when they begin thinking about backyard habitatting. More than a third of North American families are estimated to use an average of 60 pounds of birdseed each year, spending a cumulative $500 million-plus in the process.

Until quite recently such feeding efforts were largely regarded as an enjoyable hobby, but without much of a true impact on bird populations. Perhaps local populations were enhanced because of feeding efforts, but that was as far as it went.

More recent evidence, however, is beginning to point to range expansions of some species, such as the northern cardinal and house finch, directly related to increased feeding efforts. Because of the available food supply, these two species and others have extended their ranges far to the north of their traditional, natural boundaries.

For most people, winter is the season for bird feeding. They reason that the birds can find plenty of food on their own the rest of the year. This is true, but many of the birds will then find their food outside of your backyard. Year-round feeding will bring a greater variety of birds in large numbers into easy viewing range at times of the year when they are engaged in some of their most fascinating activities: courting, mating, and caring for their offspring.

In addition, many birds set up their winter ranges early in the fall by scouting for the most abundant food supplies. Those people who offer seeds consistently throughout this period will attract a much greater bird population for the winter.

ABOVE: Three different designs of feeder, each having a particular benefit, are shown here. The hanging table has a roof to keep the food dry and a low surrounding rim to keep the food in; the wire feeder is ideal for bread; and the far feeder has a curved metal baffle to prevent access by squirrels.

The type of seed offered to the birds is similarly crucial. Many of the basic commercial mixes available through grocery and department stores are filled with seeds not preferred by most backyard bird species. Any mix heavy in hulled oats, milo, peanut hearts, rice, and wheat will attract fewer birds and produce much more waste in unwanted seed. A mix heavy in black-striped sunflower seed, oil-type sunflower seed, sunflower kernels, red and white proso millet, and peanut kernels is much more attractive and useful to the birds. In addition, birds like the American goldfinch, purple finch, and house finch are particularly attracted to niger seeds.

DIFFERENT TYPES OF FEEDERS

In addition to seed preferences, different birds have feeder location preferences as well. For example, the mourning dove is a ground feeder. The American goldfinch prefers a hanging feeder with individual perches. And, the black-capped chickadee will use both of these feeders, but prefers to take one seed at a time from the feeder to a nearby shrub or tree for cracking and eating. To attract all three species into one backyard, their individual preferences must be satisfied.

Hanging or pole-mounted feeders are available in a confusing array of sizes and designs. Satisfy your personal preference, but you will enjoy the feeding experience more and the feeder will last longer if it is easy to fill with a large capacity of seed, is easy to dissemble for cleaning, has unbreakable plastic for any clear parts, has reinforced openings, and offers protection from the weather.

A specialized hanging/pole-mounted feeder is the niger seed feeder, which usually consists of a hanging tube with tiny holes to

LEFT and RIGHT: Bird feeders are the quickest way to bring many species, such as these American goldfinches, into the backyard even before your landscape elements begin to produce results. The niger seed that is especially attractive to many of the finch species, however, is relatively costly to provide for creatures such as this buck mule deer to "wolf" down in huge quantities. The deer would be equally satisfied with a much less expensive menu of sunflower seeds, cracked corn, whole corn, or even nonmeat table scraps.

accommodate the small seeds and an individual perch at each hole. Many backyard feeders prefer to offer this relatively expensive seed separately for those smaller bird species that relish it, rather than as part of the mix in their more general feeders where much of the special seed would be wasted.

Ground feeders range from simply a cleared area of soil or low grass, where seed is spread for the birds, to platforms raised on legs a foot or two off the ground. On-ground feeding should encompass an area of 8 feet or so in diameter to allow large flocks to feed at one time and avoid conflicts generally caused by more limited and cramped conditions. Raised platforms should have raised edges to prevent a lot of wasted seed. Whatever design you choose, mix some cracked corn with your normal seed mix for added bird variety and numbers.

A third feeder type is the suet feeder. These are filled with the hard fat found around beef kidneys and loins, and commonly available from butcher shops. The treat, which offers the birds a welcome source of quick high energy, can be held in small wire cages, nylon mesh bags, or a short section of log drilled with several 1-inch-diameter holes. The feeder should be hung or attached to the side of a tree or pole. This type of feeder is especially attractive to woodpeckers.

Birds will eat suet year-round, but in temperatures of more than 70°F it quickly becomes rancid and harmful to them.

In addition to the seed and suet feeders that most people think of in connection with bird feeding, you might want to offer something special for the insect-eaters, such as the nuthatches. Many insects, such as mealworms and crickets, are available year-round from bait and pet shops, and biological supply houses. Such food is relatively expensive, and generally reserved for a few special treats throughout the winter.

A much cheaper method is simply to collect a large supply of live insects in the summer and fall and freeze them in large plastic bags. Thaw them out and add them to your platform feeder or the side of a tree trunk throughout the winter.

Insect-eaters also will welcome non-insect, but high-protein foods. Bits of cheese, bacon, meat, or dry dog food are all effective. Peanut butter mixed with an equal amount of corn meal, to prevent caking and clogging in the birds' mouths and throats, can be spread on tree trunks and limbs.

Birds also need grit to digest their food throughout the year, and during periods of severe ice or snow this may be difficult for them to locate. A pan of sand particles that can be purchased in pet shops and crumbled bits of eggshell will be much appreciated.

Some of the most common backyard birds and their preferences are given in the table.

While most fruit- and seed-bearing plants will provide feeding wildlife with ready-made cover, you will need to place feeders in close proximity to trees, shrubs, and wildflower/grass patches.

In addition, if your efforts include wildlife other than birds, or birds such as the ring-necked pheasant that prefer to travel by ground, you will want to provide travel routes to and from the feeding sites. These can include hedgerows, fencerows, and rock walls.

A specialized feeder that has come into vogue in recent years, and for good reason, is the Christmas tree for wildlife. This is an evergreen "decorated" with suet-seed-grit balls, peanut butter-seed-grit balls, suet, bits of fruit, nut meats, berries and popcorn strings, and the like.

If you are committed enough to make the effort, the wildlife Christmas tree is an excellent way to introduce non-habitatters in the neighborhood to the wonders of wildlife in the backyard. Position the tree on the front lawn in place of some of your normal decorations. The brightness and life that this array of food attracts during what can be a dull, lifeless period in the outdoors can bring many converts into the habitatter fold.

Backyard Birds and Their Favorite Foods

* G – Ground, H – Hanging, HM – Hummingbird, P – Pole, PL – Platform, S – Suet
** BS – Black-striped sunflower seed, C – Cracked corn, F – Bits of fruit, M – Any millet seed, N – Niger seed, OS – Oil-type sunflower seed, P – Whole peanuts in shell, PK – Peanut kernels, S – Suet, SW – Sugar water or commercial hummingbird mixture, W – White proso millet

COMMON NAME	SCIENTIFIC NAME	FEEDER TYPE*	FOOD PREFERENCE**
American goldfinch	Carduelis tristis	H	N OS
American robin	Turdus migratorius	G	F
Black-capped chickadee	Parus atricapillus	H P G S	S OS
Black-chinned hummingbird	Archilochus alexandri	HM	SW
Blue jay	Cyanocitta cristata	H P G S	P C OS S
Brewer's blackbird	Euphagus cyanocephalus	G	C W
Brown-headed cowbird	Molothrus ater	G	C
Brown thrasher	Toxostoma rufum	G	F
Bushtit	Psaltriparus minimus	G	OS
Cardinal	Cardinalis cardinalis	H G	BS OS F
Carolina chickadee	Parus carolinensis	H P G S	OS S
Cedar waxwing	Bombycilla cedrorum	H	F
Chipping sparrow	Spizella passerina	G S	BS C S
Common crow	Corvus brachyrhynchos	G	C
Common flicker	Colaptes auratus	G H P S	BS S
Common grackle	Quiscalus quiscula	G S	BS C S
Dark-eyed junco	Junco hyemalis	G	OS BS
Downy woodpecker	Picoides pubescens	S P	S BS
Eastern phoebe	Sayornis phoebe	PL	F
European starling	Sturnus vulgaris	G	C
Fox sparrow	Passerella iliaca	G	BS W
Gray catbird	Dumetella carolinensis	PL	F
Hairy woodpecker	Picoides villosus	S H P	BS S
House finch	Carpodacus mexicanus	H P G	N OS W F
House sparrow	Passer domesticus	G	C W
Mockingbird	Mimus polyglottos	S H P	F S
Mourning dove	Zenaida macroura	G	C M OS
Northern oriole	Icterus galbula	S H	F S
Pine siskin	Carduelis pinus	H	M N OS BS
Purple finch	Carpodacus purpureus	H	BS OS
Red-bellied woodpecker	Melanerpes carolinus	S	S

COMMON NAME	SCIENTIFIC NAME	FEEDER*	FOOD**
Red-breasted nuthatch	*Sitta canadensis*	H P	BS F
Red-winged blackbird	*Agelaius phoeniceus*	G S	C M S
Ring-necked pheasant	*Phasianus colchicus*	G	C
Ruby-throated hummingbird	*Archilochus colubris*	HM	SW
Rufous-sided towhee	*Pipilo erythrophthalmus*	G	C P
Scrub jay	*Aphelocoma coerulescens*	H G S	BS C S
Song sparrow	*Melospiza melodia*	S G	S BS C W
Tree sparrow	*Spizella arborea*	G	BS C W
Tufted titmouse	*Parus bicolor*	H G S	BS PK F S
White-breasted nuthatch	*Sitta carolinensis*	H P S	BS OS S
White-crowned sparrow	*Zonotrichia leucophrys*	G	BS C W
White-throated sparrow	*Zonotrichia albicollis*	G	C PK W
Wood thrush	*Hylocichla mustelina*	G	C

squirrel baffle

hanging tube feeder

bin feeder

strung food items

platform feeding table

ABOVE and RIGHT: Literally hundreds of bird feeder designs are available commercially. When we factor in the many homemade types, such as this suet-draped cone, the number rises into the thousands. Design matters little to the birds, unless it somehow thwarts their advance or threatens their stability while perching.

ABOVE: Bird feeders and feeders for other wildlife are available in many different designs. The basic types shown here (from top) are the hanging tube feeder (ideal for feeding expensive thistle seed to smaller birds like finches), the bin feeder (a homemade version is shown), large food items strung and hung, and a platform feeding table.

SPECIAL CONSIDERATIONS FOR HUMMINGBIRDS

ABOVE: Tubular flowers, such as those of columbine (*Aquilegia* spp.), are prime attractions for hummingbirds. The tiny hummers are especially adapted to tap these flower types as a source of nectar. Different shades of red are the preferred colors, which is why many hummingbird feeders are this color.

HUMMINGBIRDS NEED SOME special consideration. Seed-filled feeders and water-filled baths – the offerings that attract nearly all other species – are simply ignored. But hummers are special enough for countless habitatters to go the extra distance.

The key to attracting hummers is flowers. Many designs of sugar-water feeders are available and the tiny birds will use them. But a selection from the flowers listed in the accompanying table is really all that's needed.

Flowers of many sorts will attract hummers. But, as has been stated before, red is the color. Orange follows closely. And a tubular or trumpet shape is preferred over other blossom designs.

Long-blooming species selected to provide flowers throughout late spring, summer, and early fall will bring hummers daily while they are residents in the region. The tiny birds winter south of the United States.

Of course, a hummingbird feeder or two will further enhance the attractiveness of your backyard to these birds, which feature prominently among the sweet tooths of the animal kingdom.

Even the cheapest models will attract some birds, but they generally cannot be taken apart for cleaning. This is a major drawback, as hummingbird feeders must be cleaned every two or three days to avoid build-ups of deadly bacteria and fungus. So, look for those that can be disassembled and clean them thoroughly with a 50:50 mixture of vinegar and hot water. Perches are not necessary on a hummingbird feeder, but the color red is advisable.

Recipes for hummingbird nectar are as numerous as those for sour-dough bread. In general, a mixture of 1 part sugar to 4 to 6 parts

HUMMER FEEDER

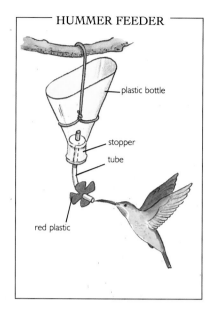

plastic bottle

stopper

tube

red plastic

water, boiled for 1 to 2 minutes, will serve the birds nicely. Do not add food coloring, but add red to the outside of the feeder device rather than to the food. In this way, the birds will not be ingesting anything artificial that they really don't need.

Place your feeders in the back-yard early each spring to attract and hold the hummers as they arrive from their annual northward migration. Maintain the feeders so long as the birds are using them. If you've encouraged several birds over the summer you will notice when they leave the area.

You can expect several other species to use your hummingbird feeders. Some, like ants, bees, and wasps, are not desirable. A smear of salad oil around the feeder opening will thwart them. Others, like sapsuckers and orioles, will be more acceptable, and they won't interfere with the hummers.

Plants for Hummingbirds

* A – Annual, B – Biennial, P – Perennial, S – Shrub, V – Vine

BOTANICAL NAME	COMMON NAME	BLOOM SEASON	HEIGHT (IN.)	USDA HARDINESS ZONES	LIFE CYCLE*
Antirrhinum majus	common snapdragon	mid-summer – first frost	18–24	5–10	A
Aquilegia canadensis	wild columbine	May–June	12–18	3–9	P
Campsis radicans	trumpet vine	mid-July	84–144	5–10	V
Chaenomeles japonica	Japanese flowering quince	mid-May	48–72	5–9	S
Dianthus x allwoodii	Allwood pink	all summer	12	7	B
Fuchsia x hybrida	fuchsia	all summer	24–60	5–10	A
Hemerocallis spp.	daylilies	July–Aug.	30–40	3–9	P
Heuchera sanguinea	coral bells	all summer	16–20	4–9	P
Hibiscus moscheutos	common rose mallow	Aug.–Sept.	60–72	4–9	P
Lilium spp.	lilies	June–Sept.	36–72	3–10	P
Lupinus spp.	lupines	May–June	24–60	4–7	P
Monarda didyma	bee balm	July–Aug.	24–36	4–9	P
Nicotiana alata 'Grandiflora'	flowering tobacco	all summer	15	6–10	A
Penstemon barbatus	common beardtongue	June–July	24–36	4–9	P
Petunia x hybrida 'Multiflora'	petunia	all summer	12–18	4–10	A
Phlox paniculata	garden phlox	July–Aug.	18–24	3–9	P
Physostegia virginiana	obedient plant	Aug.–Oct.	36–42	3–10	P
Salvia splendens	scarlet sage	early summer – first frost	8–16	5–10	A
Tropaeolum majus	nasturtium	all summer	12	4–10	A
Weigela florida	old-fashioned weigela	late May	to 108	6–10	V

ABOVE: A hummingbird feeder is easily made from the spout of a plastic bottle, the stopper and tube from a small-animal watering bottle, and red plastic, cut to look like a flower.

RIGHT: In place of flowers, hummingbird feeders filled with sugar-water mixtures will bring the little birds into close proximity to the house.

NESTBOXES AND NESTING SITES

BIRDHOUSES OR, MORE accurately nestboxes, have been a part of backyard wildlife habitats since well before they were known as such. A few old pieces of wood nailed together, a hole drilled or cut in the front, and the whole affair nailed to some nearby tree has been a rite of childhood for generations.

Recent years have brought more focus and more sophistication to the pursuit. Many designs of nestboxes are available commercially. Some are even designed for wildlife other than birds. But, ultimately, the true function of any nestbox is simulation of the cavity in a tree that a particular creature would choose for nesting. Select a box for the specific species that you want to attract. The table on page 97 covers some of the most common backyard species.

Certain species also prefer to nest in specific environments. Boxes placed in these locations stand a better chance of attracting use by the intended species. For instance, the American kestrel prefers open agricultural areas; barn owls like a sheltered location, such as the inside of a barn wall, within a mile of grasslands, meadows, or woodland-field edge; barn swallows nest on house or garage walls; the barred owl needs woodlands; a nestbox for bats is best placed on the side of a tree or house where it receives maximum heat from sun and protection from wind; black-capped chickadees nest near evergreens and at wood lot edges; the deer mouse prefers wooded

areas; and eastern bluebirds like meadows, backyards, and grasslands near mixed hardwood forests. The eastern phoebe prefers to nest near water, while the great-crested flycatcher enjoys an orchard- or park-like setting; house wrens will choose a box under the eaves of a house or in a tree; mourning doves like evergreens; the northern flicker likes wood lots, orchards, and edges of crop fields. Nuthatches need wooded areas, while the purple martin requires a box at least 40 feet from the nearest tree

and close to open water.

Raccoons like their nest boxes on a tree and sheltered from winds, and screech owls prefer wood lots and orchards. Squirrels need to nest in a wooded area; tree swallows seek out open lands near water; the tufted titmouse and the white-footed mouse prefer wooded areas while the wood duck needs a wetland area or one along a waterway; woodpeckers will only use nest boxes in wood lots.

Some species will make quicker use of nestboxes if wood chips –

LEFT: A recent addition to many backyard habitats across much of North America is the bat box. The flying mammals have taken to the boxes as readily as birds have done for centuries, adding a whole new dimension to the backyard habitat. Fears that the small creatures attack human heads are unfounded.

BELOW: Purple martins will make ready use of imitations of the gourd-based colony nests that Native Americans used for generations to attract the insect-eating birds to the vicinity of their crops. Commercial versions are available, but the nesting structures can be made from dried, hollowed gourd shells.

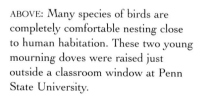

ABOVE: Many species of birds are completely comfortable nesting close to human habitation. These two young mourning doves were raised just outside a classroom window at Penn State University.

not sawdust – are provided for them in the cavity. Some of these are the American kestrel, black-capped chickadee, flicker (fill the box to the top), screech owl, tufted titmouse, white-breasted nuthatch, wood duck, and woodpecker.

In addition to these specific requirements, there are some common considerations for all nestboxes.

1 One side of the roof should be hinged to allow for easy cleaning each year.

2 A half-dozen ¼-inch holes should be drilled in the floor to allow for drainage. Similar holes should be drilled near the top of the two sides to provide ventilation.

3 The roof should overhang at least 2 inches over the entrance hole to shelter the interior from rain and to keep predators from reaching in.

4 A perch on a nestbox will attract house sparrows and European starlings, but does nothing to enhance use by other, more desirable species.

5 The floor should be recessed ¼ inch up from the bottom of the sides to prevent rain from seeping inside.

6 Avoid metals and plastics as nestbox materials, and stains and wood finishes that contain pentachlorophenol, green preservative, and creosote.

7 If mice, squirrels, bees, or wasps set up housekeeping in a nestbox intended for birds, simply remove their nest or allow them use of the box and put up an extra one for the birds. Take care when removing a wasp nest or bee hive.

With the nestboxes you may want to offer a few extras that will make nesting conditions in your backyard even more attractive. Many bird species will use bits of yarn and hair offered to them in a mesh-net bag hung from a tree limb. Horsehair offers a special attraction for song sparrows. American robins will return repeatedly to a mud-filled depression that you can make simply by keeping the area moist.

BELOW: A wide variety of cavity-nesting birds will make use of this basic nesting box design. The size of the box and the entrance hole must be varied to fit the size of the intended occupant, as detailed on the chart opposite. A hinged roof will make your after-use cleanings of the box much easier. Drainage holes in the floor help to keep the occupants and their nestlings healthier by quickly removing any water that does get inside.

BIRDHOUSE BASICS

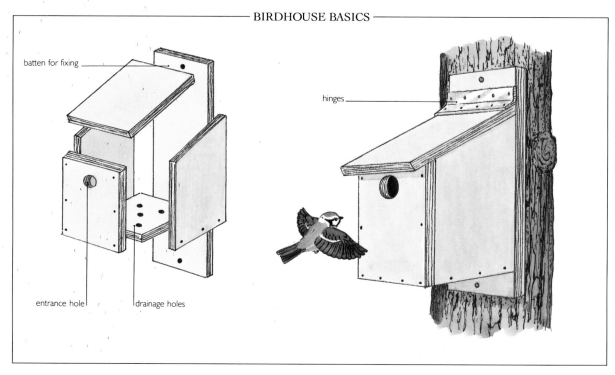

batten for fixing

entrance hole   drainage holes

hinges

GOING NATIVE

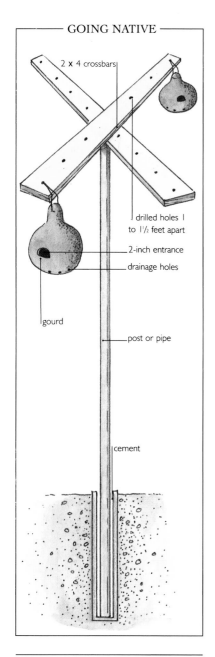

2 x 4 crossbars

drilled holes 1 to 1½ feet apart

2-inch entrance

drainage holes

gourd

post or pipe

cement

ABOVE: For an unusual backyard feature, you might want to follow the lead of native Americans, who hung collections of large hollowed-out gourds in their gardens to attract insect-eating purple martin colonies. The post should be 10 to 18 feet tall.

Nestbox Requirements

COMMON NAME	SCIENTIFIC NAME	FLOOR (IN.)	DEPTH (IN.)	ENTRANCE ABOVE FLOOR (IN.)	ENTRANCE DIAMETER (IN.)	ABOVE GROUND (FT.)
BIRDS						
American kestrel	*Falco sparverius*	11x11	12	9–12	3x4	20–30
American robin	*Turdus migratorius*	6x8	8	no sides		6–15
Barn owl	*Tyto alba*	10x18	15–18	4	6	12–18
Barn swallow	*Hirundo rustica*	6x6	6	no sides		8–12
Black-capped chickadee	*Parus atricapillus*	4x4	8–10	6–8	1⅛	6–15
Carolina wren	*Thryothorus ludovicianus*	4x4	6–8	1–6	1½	6–10
Common flicker	*Colaptes auratus*	7x7	16–18	14–16	2½	6–20
Crested flycatcher	*Myiarchus crinitus*	6x6	8	6	2	8–20
Downy woodpecker	*Picoides pubescens*	4x4	9–12	6–8	1¼	6–20
Eastern bluebird	*Sialia sialis*	5x5	8	6	1½	5
European starling	*Sturnus vulgaris*	6x6	16–18	14–16	2	10–25
Hairy woodpecker	*Picoides villosus*	6x6	12–15	9–12	1½	12–20
House finch	*Carpodacus mexicanus*	6x6	6	4	2	6–12
House wren	*Troglodytes aedon*	4x4	8–10	1–6	1¼	6–10
Purple martin	*Progne subis*	6x6	6	1	2½	10–20
Red-headed woodpecker	*Melanerpes erythrocephalus*	6x6	12	10	2	10–20
Screech owl	*Otus asio*	8x8	12–15	9–12	3	10–30
Song sparrow	*Melospiza melodia*	6x6	6	no sides		1–3
Tree swallow	*Iridoprocne bicolor*	5x5	6–8	5–6	1½	6–16
Tufted titmouse	*Parus bicolor*	4x4	8–10	6–8	1¼	6–15
White-breasted nuthatch	*Sitta carolinensis*	4x4	8–10	6–8	1¼	12–20
Wood duck	*Aix sponsa*	10x18	10–24	12–16	4	10–20
MAMMALS						
Bat*	Several species	6x8	14	at rear base	¾	12–15
White-footed mouse	*Peromyscus maniculatus*	4x5	8–11	6	1¼	5–10
Raccoon	*Procyon lotor*	16x18	30	25	5x9	7–20
Squirrel	Several species	10x11	24	20	3 (on side)	12–20

* At the center inside the bat box, an additional upright board equal to the width of the box (8 inches) should extend from the roof to 2 inches above the floor. This provides a roosting surface.

MAMMALS, LARGE AND SMALL

SMALLER MAMMALS SUCH AS chipmunks, squirrels, rabbits, moles, and voles will be attracted into your habitat through everything you've done to this point. Some, such as opossums, raccoons, and skunks, will begin naturally to include the ready sources of food and water you've created in their regular nightly rounds. However, for many of the larger mammals – from opossum-size and up – there are some specific things that you can add to your habitat mix. Before doing any of the following things, give some thought to the dangers of animal-borne diseases, such as rabies. Realistically, the danger of incidentally attracting these troubles into your backyard is minimal, but the potential does exist.

Another preliminary consideration before you begin attempts to attract larger mammals is the location of your property. If you're situated in the middle of a highly developed community that offers very little in the way of protected travel routes for such animals, it is probably unfair to offer them incentive to risk such a trip.

One property in a wooded area along an interstate highway that I travel frequently comes to mind. Three sides of the property are surrounded by forest, seemingly an ideal location to attract a great variety of wildlife. But the fourth side borders on the interstate.

The owner places a great deal of food attractants about his property, especially corn for deer and bears. And he gets results. It is not

TOP: The only marsupial on the North American continent, the opossum, is readily attracted to the backyard with offerings of nearly any type of food, so long as that food is offered in protected but easily accessible locations. Opossums are mostly nocturnal visitors.

ABOVE: Raccoons, too, are easily attracted into the backyard habitat at night, although they can take a much more active role in availing themselves of all possible food sources – whether intended for their use or not.

uncommon to see a small herd of whitetails gathered at his feeders each day at dusk. It's not unheard of to spot a black bear occasionally as well. Unfortunately, I can't recall ever driving by that property on the interstate without spotting the remains of at least one deer that's been mowed down by the speeding traffic. And I know of at least one black bear that's been killed on that same section of highway. Obviously, the easily available food in an unsafe location is bringing the larger mammals into peril.

On the other hand, if you do have a safe location with secure travel routes, larger mammals can bring a special dimension to backyard habitat efforts. For many habitatters that I know the nightly appearance of a few deer or a fox is proof positive that they've accomplished their goals.

A salt block, available from any farm or feed supply store, is an excellent starting point for these special efforts. The various deer species across the country are the primary target of this offering, but many other species have a natural taste for the mineral.

Several companies now also offer mineral blocks that have been shown not only to attract the deer, but also to enhance the growth of antlers in the bucks. I've produced some very effective salt licks by simply dumping a container or two of common table salt onto an old stump or log and letting the rain soak it into the wood and surrounding soil.

Many of the carnivores are similarly attracted to the scraps left after fish have been cleaned – the heads, fins, and internal organs. Red fox are particularly susceptible to this treat. An uncle of mine eventually coerced an entire family of the canines to visit the edge of his backyard each evening for the leftovers from his day of trout fishing. Opossums, skunks, raccoons, and coyotes also are attracted to these and any other food scraps that you choose to leave out for them.

CAUTION: If you have domestic cats as pets you may not want to attract fox and coyote into your area. Cats are high on their list of prey species. There also are many reports of coyote attacks on dogs.

The powerful sweet tooth of both raccoons and black bears can be exploited to encourage them to make your backyard part of their regular nightly rounds, if your backyard borders on their normal habitats. Honey or sweet syrups of all types dribbled into the crevices of a stump or log will hold their attention until the last drop has been licked up. In addition, Canadian hunting guides have discovered that old doughnuts offer a strong attraction for bears.

CAUTION: Do not attempt to attract bears if there is any possibility of them becoming a nuisance or a danger to neighbors.

THE DIRT HOLE

covering soil

rock

bait

ABOVE: If night prowlers are visiting your backyard but you haven't seen them, a dirt hole will record their tracks. Bury a small piece of fish or meat at the base of a rock and sift the soil back over it.

LEFT: Squirrels are probably the most common mammal in backyard habitats from coast to coast.

ROCKY MOUNTAIN GARDEN

LIVING ON 15 ACRES OF THE
FLATHEAD INDIAN RESERVATION IN
THE FOOTHILLS AT THE CONTINENTAL
DIVIDE, MARY KEAST (ABOVE) HAS
THE "WILDEST" OF ANY OF OUR
FEATURED BACKYARD HABITATS. THE
OLD HOMESTEAD, COMPLETE WITH
APPLE AND PLUM ORCHARDS PLANTED
IN THE 1930s, IS LOCATED ABOUT
3½ MILES OUTSIDE THE TOWN OF
ST. IGNATIUS, MONTANA.

TOP: In Mary Keast's Montana
neighborhood, backyards take on a
whole new dimension. Her own
property is 15 acres, filled with a wide
variety of volunteering wildflowers,
like this draba species, ABOVE.
Although Keast has done much to
enhance the property for wildlife,
natural processes have contributed
even more to the effort.

Bears – usually black bears,
although grizzlies are regular
inhabitants of adjacent national
forest lands – are not uncommon
visitors in late spring and fall.
One cinnamon-phase black bear
remained on the property for two
weeks a few years back.

The Keasts adopt a live-and-let-
live attitude, which is enhanced by
excitement over such a visitor: "If
you don't bother them, they won't
bother you. And, after all, they'll
be gone in a couple of weeks."
Similarly, because of poor salmon
runs in Glacier National Park

LEFT: Heavily overgrown patches of wildflowers, such as this area dominated by oxeye daisies and weeds, attract nearly all wildlife species.

during the past few years, elks, badgers and coyotes will turn up on the property regularly during the winter. And bald eagles have been seen from the backyard.

While most backyard wildlife gardeners won't be able to attract such exciting species, we wanted to include this example to encourage those lucky enough to have the grounds and a suitable location to go ahead and develop their habitat. And the advice of Mary Keast for new backyard wildlife gardeners applies equally well to any situation: "Take a look at what you've got already. Leave one part of it wild. Don't plow the whole thing up. Don't mow the whole thing down. Don't cut the trees down.

"If you can't identify something on the property, before you remove it get somebody in, like a county extension agent, who can identify it for you. Live with it for one year at least, to become familiar with the birds and animals which would certainly be absent for part of the year."

Keast keeps a journal of her observations, something that many other veterans maintain religiously. This is an excellent idea for the beginner as well, allowing him or her to build up a personal database quickly and accurately.

"We probably have the messiest

plot of any of our neighbors," says Keast. "They keep their fence rows trimmed and the brush cut around their homes." But the Keast property also benefits from its wildlife population. After pointing out that "It wasn't very buggy this summer at all," she notes that "Several pairs of bluebirds and a pair each of flycatchers, violet-green swallows, and tree swallows nested within the habitat this year."

Bluebirds have made a strong comeback on the Keast property in response to the bluebird houses that have been placed about the grounds. This is part of a national story that demonstrates so clearly how a species has been helped by the efforts of thousands of wildlife gardeners and nature centers.

Similarly, on the Keast property, where heavy livestock grazing has been eliminated, the native grasses and wildflowers are in full recovery. She plans to enhance this regrowth by starting several wildflower patches for butterflies.

Of course, wild critters will bring some problems with them just by being themselves. For example, when the Keasts planted buffalo berries – a relatively rare plant in the region – a few years back, the goal was eventually to make jam. But when the plants gave their first crop of berries, the ringnecked pheasants ate them all in one day.

Water on the property is provided primarily by the large channel that runs across the grounds. In this region there are thousands of miles of such channels, developed by government agencies

BELOW: Keast has cultivated many berry-producing plants, like these currants, on her property. However, most of the crop is eaten by her wildlife guests rather than by her family. Many of these plants provide thick cover as well as food.

to collect snowmelt in the mountains and transport that water to farmlands and ranches in the valleys. On the Keast property, water runs through the channel from May to September, and this attracts several species of nesting ducks and herons.

In winter when the channel isn't running, Keast places pans of water out for the birds. She also puts out plenty of bird seed during the winter, noting that "Just before a cold spell hits, those birds are out there gobbling up the seeds."

Some of the wildlife-attracting plants in the Keast habitat:

TREES
apple, balsam poplar, cherry, crab apple, Italian plum, maple, red plum, walnut

SHRUBS AND VINES
blackberry, buffalo berry, chokecherry, columbine, currant, grape, juniper, osier dogwood

FLOWERS AND HERBS
beargrass, butter-and-eggs, cinquefoil, clover, forget-me-not, goat's beard, leafy spurge, mustard, raspberry, shooting star, snowberry, stonecrop, thistle, vetch, violet, wild grass, wild hyacinth, wild rose, wild strawberry, wild sunflower

Some of the wildlife sighted in the Keast habitat:

BIRDS
American goldfinch, American kestrel, American robin, Audubon warbler, bald eagle, black-capped chickadee, bobolink, Bohemian waxwing, Clark's nutcracker, common crow, evening grosbeak, falcon, goose (various species), great blue heron, hawk (various species), house finch, house wren, hummingbird (various species), Hungarian partridge, killdeer, lazuli bunting, loggerhead shrike, magpie, mallard, meadowlark, mountain chickadee, mourning dove, northern flicker, Oregon junco, oriole, owl (various species), phoebe, pine siskin, purple finch, raven, red-eyed vireo, red-winged blackbird, ring-necked pheasant, ruffed grouse, rufous-sided towhee, sharp-tailed grouse, snipe, sparrow, Stellar's jay, Townsend's solitaire, tree swallow, turkey vulture, violet-green swallow, western bluebird, western flycatcher, western kingbird, western tanager, wild turkey, woodpecker (various species), yellow-headed blackbird

MAMMALS
badger, black bear, coyote, elk, gopher, mink, mole, mouse, raccoon, shrew, vole, white-tailed deer

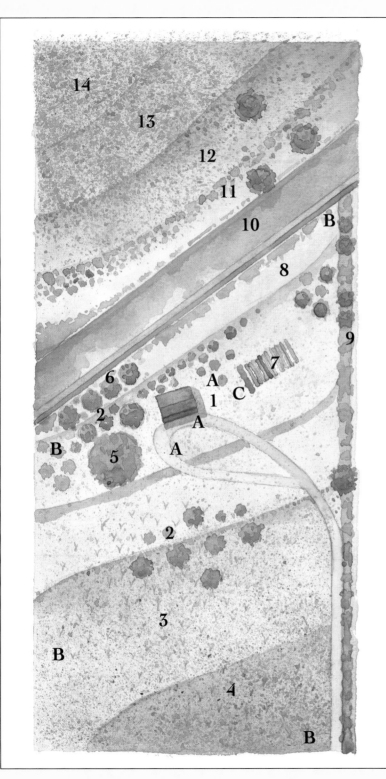

house finch

KEAST HABITAT
1 house and driveway
2 orchard
3 grass-clover pasture, with scattered areas of wild rose thickets
4 possible area for adding pond and drainage ditches at later date
5 balsam poplar
6 concrete-lined contour ditch
7 garden with rows of buffalo berry bushes in front
8 wild roses, chokeberry, thistles, forget-me-nots
9 chokeberries, dogwood, red and white blackcurrants, wild roses, snowberries, and thistle along entire length
10 canal
11 leafy spurge, native grasses, wildflowers
12 native grasses, wildflowers
13 good native grass, deep soil
14 sparse native grass, thin soil

A feeder
B bluebird house
C well

ABOVE: Although chokecherry leaves and fruit pits are poisonous to humans, many wildlife species feed heavily on the ripe fruits.

AROUND THE YEAR IN THE BACKYARD HABITAT

ALTHOUGH NATURE RARELY follows any exact schedule, there is a general pattern for those involved with backyard habitats that can be seen across much of North America.

WINTER

The southern portion of the continent plays host to many of the bird species that migrate from more northerly regions. Some birds, however, remain in their northern ranges throughout the winter.

Keep the feeders filled, both in the South and North. In the colder regions, consider setting out a pan of warm (not hot) water for the birds' use, until it freezes, or keep the water heater active in the bird bath.

Place your cut Christmas tree in a corner of the backyard as a temporary (into early spring) shelter for wildlife. Many species now are facing their most trying time of the year. Only a few creatures spend the entire winter in hibernation or states close to hibernation. Shelter and food are much sought after.

In the North, nearly all insect, amphibian, and reptile species will not be seen again for several months. Unexpected warm periods, however, may bring some out of hibernation.

Use the seed catalogs that begin to arrive now to start planning this year's additions to the backyard habitat. Another indoor activity to break the doldrums is to build nest-boxes and birdhouses.

In late winter, position your new nestboxes and birdhouses. Clean out those already in place. Make repairs and replacements as necessary. Some bird migrants already are returning in the North.

On warmer days, get out into your backyard to look for any signals that spring is just around the corner. Check grates and screening over chimneys, air vents, and little-used windows to make certain that they are still secure against wildlife in search of a protected nesting site.

ABOVE: The first few hours of daylight after a night of light snow are a favorite time for many backyard habitatters. Normally undetected comings and goings will be revealed by trails, such as this made by a passing striped skunk in the backyard of a central New York property.

ABOVE: A well-designed and maintained backyard habitat will bring a never-ending array of special events into view. This female cardinal was observed in central Pennsylvania, assisting the parents in the brooding of a nestful of American robin chicks. It is believed she lost her own chicks and this was her response to that loss.

SPRING

Keep the feeders filled and your water source in active operation. Feeders for hummingbirds, butterflies, and moths should be started in late spring. If you've decided to add an above-ground water source, now is the time to do it. Early spring is also the time for cleaning out existing water sources.

The return of migrant bird species is now in high gear. Offer nest-building materials such as bits of yarn and strands of hair.

In late spring, feeders can be taken down. But they will provide much more entertainment if kept filled throughout the year.

Late spring is a peak time for wildlife activity. Don't get so caught up in your yard work that you allow no time to sit back and enjoy the results of your habitat. However, there is much to be done at this time as well.

Prune shrubs that have passed the flowering stage, but be careful not to expose active nests nor to prune fruit-bearers too closely. Clean out old growth from perennial areas. It's planting time. Be careful of insects, amphibians, and reptiles that spent the winter in and under plant debris. Many species now are beginning to emerge.

SUMMER

If you've decided to add an in-ground water source, the soil should now be dry enough to get started.

In the garden, struggles with pests are under way in earnest. If you don't already have one, start a compost pile.

RIGHT: A Christmas tree for the birds can really cheer up an otherwise bleak and colorless time of the year outdoors. Many treats for the birds can be fashioned into natural, edible ornaments, such as a string of popcorn or a suet-covered pine cone.

LEFT: Brightly blooming flowers and courting, mating, and nesting songbirds are two of the special wildlife qualities that mark each spring in the backyard habitat. This is the most colorful and active time of the year in the natural world as life renews itself with vigor.

Hummingbird, butterfly, and moth feeders should be attracting steady business. Bits of fruit, including oranges and bananas, will attract birds such as orioles and thrashers.

Gather wild fruits and berries, where you have permission, and store them for use as wildlife food through the winter. Do this outside of your own backyard habitat, leaving the fruits hanging on your plants.

In late summer some bird species will begin their migrations southward; others will begin staging for later trips.

FALL

Bird migration is under way in earnest in early fall. Insects, amphibians, and reptiles are becoming much less common, as they seek out their winter refuge. Hibernating and semi-hibernating mammals are stockpiling for their winter inactivity. All other mammals also are building up their body resources for winter.

Hummingbird, butterfly, and moth feeders can be discontinued early in fall. Continue gathering wild fruits and berries, where you have permission, and store them for winter use. If you discontinued feeding for the spring and summer, it's time to start up again.

If your water source is less than 2 feet deep, the plants and animals should be relocated late this month. Relocate existing perennials and plant new ones as desired. In the North, drain any water source that is less than 2 feet deep or begin use of water heaters.

Plant spring-flowering bulbs. Add your raked leaves to the compost pile. Clean out annuals and vegetables killed off by the first frost. Prepare ornamental plants for winter.

In late fall, step up your feeding efforts, with the addition of suet and peanut-butter feeders. Keep the water source available and, if necessary, heated. Prune deciduous trees and shrubs. Mulch with straw as needed. Build on existing brush-piles or create new ones.

When you decorate for Christmas, consider including a Christmas tree for wildlife. Think of backyard habitat-related gifts for the holidays.

ABOVE and RIGHT: The location of your property within the larger environment of your neighborhood will place some limits on how much you can achieve with your backyard habitat. A location close to agricultural or meadow-type lands will increase the likelihood of attracting species like the ring-necked pheasant. On the other hand, even ornamental plantings, such as this snapdragon (*Antirrhinum* spp.) bed, also have some wildlife value. The well-balanced backyard habitat provides a blend of human and wildlife uses in harmony with one another.

–IDENTIFICATION–
AND OBSERVATION

NOW THAT YOU'VE DEVELOPED YOUR BACKYARD
HABITAT, IT'S TIME TO STOP AND SMELL THE
DANDELIONS. YOUR ENJOYMENT OF THE WILDLIFE
THAT YOU'RE NOW ATTRACTING INTO THE
BACKYARD WILL BE GREATLY ENHANCED BY USING
SOME OF THE TECHNIQUES EMPLOYED BY
PROFESSIONAL WILDLIFE OBSERVERS. HERE IS AN
INTRODUCTION TO SOME OF THESE.

RIGHT: Special moments, such as this
white-footed mouse nursing her
young, will fill your backyard habitat.
But only careful observation will
reveal them to you. Journal-keeping
and photography are two skills that
will enhance such discoveries and save
them for years to come, even when the
many habitat events have begun to
blur in your memory.

OBSERVING AND RECORDING

YOU, TOO, WILL MAKE discoveries on a par with the stale-doughnut-bearing Canadian hunting guides. You probably will make many more discoveries about your wildlife and habitat than you can imagine right now. It's practically impossible for anyone to observe wildlife in his or her habitat for any length of time without gaining some insights.

Unless you keep a journal of all your observations, many or most of your discoveries will soon fade from memory and be lost. Certainly you will not spot as many trends without this written memory-jogger.

Don't worry about the formality of your journal. It doesn't need to live up to scientific standards. Find a simple format that will be useful to you and that you will stay with.

Some elements customarily found in a habitatter's journals are the date and time of the observation, general or specific weather information at the time, the species involved, and the behavior you observed (particularly behavior that relates to elements of your habitat). A simple backyard weather station, available from many scientific and novelty mail-order houses, can be valuable in determining specific weather information.

Include sketches as much as possible. This effort will force you to look more closely for details and better your overall skills as an observer. Don't be shy about your lack of formal art training or your self-imposed lack of artistic skill.

ABOVE: Photography will enable you to capture special moments for future reference as well as prompt you to observe more closely.

You need never show your work to anyone else.

One bit of formality that I would suggest you adopt from the beginning of your journal is an indexing system. It may not seem like a necessity at first. But after you have filled a couple of dozen journals, how else are you going to find and link all your observations about birds' use of a particular species of plant in your wildflower patch?

Index your journals on index cards. They are easy to expand and alter. Make your index as simple as a card for each major plant species in your habitat, with the date for each observation involving that plant written on the card in chronological order. Or, you might want to have a card for each wildlife species seen in your backyard.

PHOTOGRAPHY

Space limitations will not permit a thorough discussion of photographic equipment and techniques. You will have to rely on other books and magazines as well as your own investigations through camera shops to decide what equipment is right for you. A book that is easy to understand and thorough on the specific topic of wildlife photography is *A Practical Guide to Photographing American Wildlife*, which is available from the author, Joe McDonald, Rural Route 2, Box 1095, McClure, PA 17841.

The average snapshot camera offered for the hobbyist is almost always inadequate for wildlife photography. Without a great deal of blind luck, you will never get anything close to those photos you admire in wildlife magazines; most animals will simply be small blobs.

The 35 millimeter single lens reflex (SLR) camera, with a wide selection of interchangeable special lenses, is the standard in professional wildlife photography today. And the good news is that this equipment is now within many people's price range.

A telephoto lens is the means to getting those impressive shot-filling close-ups you really want. A telephoto lens does for the camera and film what binoculars do for the eyes: It magnifies the images. It allows you to get "close" to your subject without pressing so closely that you will scare it off. You will need a lens in the range of 300 to 400 millimeters.

BINOCULARS

To make the kinds of detailed observations needed to produce a really useful journal or simply to enjoy more fully the wildlife that you attract into your backyard habitat, a good pair of binoculars is indispensable.

A wide assortment is available in most any well-stocked outdoor shop or mail-order catalog, and at an equally wide range of prices. Remember that price in high-quality optics is usually a good indicator of the relative quality of a product. Compare features of those binoculars available within your price range and make your selection accordingly.

Some of the specialized terms you will encounter:

Power is the magnification factor offered by the binoculars. The number before the "x" is the power. It is the number of times the binoculars magnify whatever you are looking at. For example, 7x magnifies the image seven times. Most backyard wildlife watchers prefer 7x or 8x.

Objective lens refers to the size of the lens. It is expressed by the second half of a set of numbers, such as 6x30 or 7x35, imprinted on the housing. It is the number after the "x," generally expressed in millimeters. The larger this number, the more light-gathering capacity is available in the lens.

Brightness is the bright area offered through the exit pupil of the binocular lens. You can determine this factor by dividing the size of the objective lens by the power.

ABOVE: Telephoto lenses are needed to capture the more interesting, detailed close-ups that you see in books and magazines. And tripods provide the steadiness required to shoot these images with a degree of sharpness.

For example, a 6x30 binocular has an exit pupil of 5 millimeters. Exit pupils of 2 to 4 millimeters are recommended for bright light situations, 4 or 5 millimeters for shaded areas and more than 5 millimeters for use at dawn or dusk.

Lens coating is the film applied to optics to reduce the amount of light reflection and glare within the lens. You can check this by holding the binoculars under fluorescent light and looking at the objective lenses. If they are coated properly, they will appear purple or amber. If they are not, they will appear white.

Field of view is the width of the image you see through the binoculars. It is usually expressed as the width in feet when viewed at 1,000 yards. It is often printed on the housing as degrees. Multiply this number by 52.5 and you know the field of view in feet. Some wildlife watchers prefer wider fields of view to permit easier and quicker spotting of their target. Others prefer lesser fields of view to eliminate extraneous details.

Center-focus will permit focusing on much closer objects than will systems in which each eyepiece must be focused individually.

INTRODUCTION TO BACKYARD SPECIES

This section of the book introduces some of the species of wildlife that you'll be most likely to find in your backyard habitat. The species are grouped into their six taxonomic classes.

Insects This is the largest class of animals. It also is the most populous group in your backyard, although you probably will never be aware of all of its members. On the other hand, some are quite visible, such as the butterflies; or audible, such as the crickets; or pesky, such as the gnats.

Every mature insect has three body parts: head, thorax, and abdomen; two antennae; a pair of mandibles; and three pairs of legs. Most insects reach maturity after a process of metamorphosis through several distinct and quite different stages. The insect skeleton is external and must be shed for growth to take place.

Arachnids This class of animal life is the one commonly, but mistakenly, grouped with insects. However, these spiders, scorpions, mites, and ticks are definitely distinct from insects. They have two body parts – cephalothorax and abdomen – and four pairs of legs. They usually have eight eyes.

You'll spot the occasional spider's web, particularly on dew-soaked mornings, without much effort. But you'll discover a great many more of these creatures, as they hunt their prey or wait in ambush, if you get down on your knees and look more closely on the ground.

SPECIAL TERMS

Abdomen	The posterior of the three major subdivisions of an insect's body
Antennae	Paired sensory appendages on an insect's head
Apex	Outer tip of butterfly and moth wing
Above	Refers to upper butterfly and moth wings
Bar	Mark across a feather or group of bird feathers
Below	Refers to underside of butterfly and moth wings
Cell	Central area of butterfly and moth wing
Cephalothorax	First subdivision of a spider's body, composed of head and thorax
Costa	Front margin of butterfly and moth wing
Elytra	The hardened or leathery wing(s) of beetles
Margin	Outer butterfly and moth wing edge
Median	Area halfway between base and apex of butterfly and moth wing
Nape	Hind neck of bird
Post-median line	Band below submarginal band on butterfly and moth wing
Pronotum	Dorsal surface of the prothorax
Prothorax	First segment of the thorax
Submargin	Band below marginal band on butterfly and moth wing
Stigma	Scent scale on butterfly and moth wing
Thorax	The middle of the three major subdivisions of an insect's body

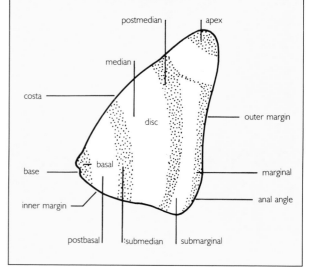

Amphibians These are most likely to be found under objects in your habitat, near your water source, and out roaming on warm, rainy nights. They need a relatively moist component to their environment at all times.

Amphibians were the first true land-dwellers, crawling up out of the oceans approximately 300 million years ago. Unlike reptiles, they have non-scaly, smooth, moist skin. Most spend their lives on land but lay their eggs in water. They are cold-blooded, but most of their other bodily systems are similar to those of the higher animals. They also display an amazing ability to regenerate lost body parts.

Reptiles Probably the most limited class of backyard guest, reptiles may appear on warm, sunny days and in open "sunning" locations, such as rocks, stone walls, wood piles, and the sides of buildings.

As a class, reptiles fall between amphibians and birds and mammals on the evolutionary scale. Most reptiles are egg-layers, although many snakes and lizards give birth to live offspring. They are cold-blooded and their bodies are covered with scales or bony plates.

Birds This group will be the most immediately visible wildlife in your backyard. Some will make their regular visits even if you do nothing extra to attract them. Of course, a great many more will come to a fully developed habitat garden.

Feathers are unique to birds. Every adult bird has feathers. In addition, bird bodies are specially adapted for flight with many hollow, fused bones. Although birds evolved from different reptilian ancestors than mammals, the two classes share many characteristics, such as being warm-blooded and having four-chambered hearts. Birds, however, share the initial development of their young inside eggs with most of the lower animals.

Mammals This is the most evolutionarily advanced class of animals and the one to which human beings belong. You will see the mammals that frequent your habitat most often between late afternoon and the first hours of daylight. They tend to do most of their moving about, feeding, and the rest of their regular routine under the cover of twilight or darkness. However, some, like squirrels, chipmunks, and woodchucks, are active during the day, and other mammals may show up at any time.

Except for the egg-laying monotremes (which include the duck-billed platypus), all mammals bear live offspring. All females have mammary glands with which to nourish their young, which are dependent upon their mother or both parents at birth. In addition to being warm-blooded and having four-chambered hearts, mammals have the most highly developed nervous systems of all the animals.

1 AMERICAN BUMBLE BEE *(Bombus pennsylvanicus)*, ½–1¼ inches, black head and behind wings, yellow abdomen, darkly tinted wings. Range: US; southern Canada. Habitat: weedy, grassy areas near wooded areas. How to attract: flowers for nectar.

2 PEA APHID *(Acyrthosiphon pisum)*, ⅛–¼ inch, soft, lime green, gelatinous body. Range: all of US and Canada. Habitat: weedy areas; beans or peas. Undesirable.

3 POTTER WASP *(Eumenes fraternus)*, ½–¾ inch, black with yellow spots and ring at end of abdomen, darkly tinted wings. Range: eastern US and Canada, west to Texas. Habitat: wooded areas and weedy areas. How to attract: nectar plants.

4 CARPENTER BEE *(Xylocopa virginica)*, ¾–1 inch, black to blue-black, very short hair on abdomen. Range: eastern US and Canada. Habitat: wooded areas and adjacent fields. How to attract: adult takes nectar from flowers.

5 YELLOW MUD DAUBER *(Scelipthron caementarium)*, 1–1¼ inches, black with yellow patterning and yellow legs, darkly tinted wings. Range: all US and Canada. Habitat: open areas with overhanging shelter for mud nests. How to attract: nectar plants.

6 BEAN APHID *(Aphis fabae)*, ¹⁄₁₂–⅛ inch, dark green to greenish black, adult is winged. Range: all of US and Canada. Habitat: weedy areas; beans, beets, peas or spinach. Undesirable.

7 RED ANT *(Formica spp.)*, ⅛–½ inch, red to brown, darker at abdomen, waist between thorax and abdomen. Range: northern US; southern Canada. Habitat: wooded areas. How to attract: flowers for nectar.

8 YELLOW JACKET *(Vespula spp.)*, ½–⅝ inch, striped black and yellow or white, heavily tinted wings, narrow waist. Range: all US and Canada. Habitat: wooded areas and adjacent weedy areas. Generally seen as a pest species.

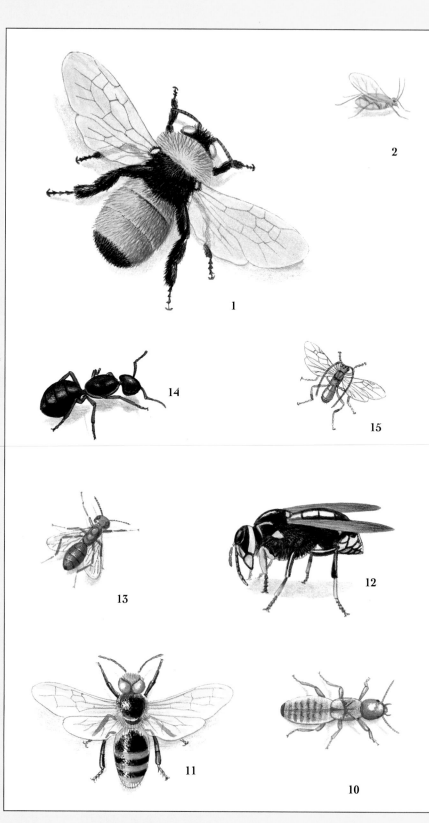

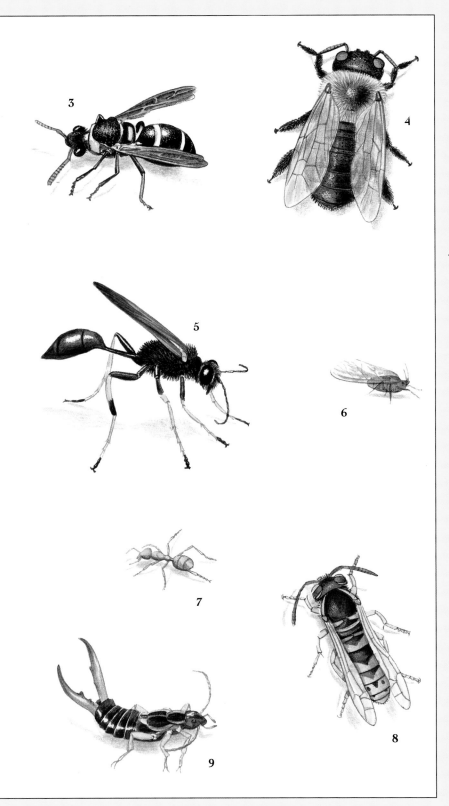

9 EUROPEAN EARWIG
(Forficula auricularia), ³/₈–⁵/₈ inch, red-brown body and forceps with yellow antennae, legs, elytra; short wings. Range: northeastern US; eastern Canada. Habitat: damp, sheltered areas. A garden pest.

10 TERMITE *(Order Isoptera)*, ¹/₂–1 inch, brown to black with orange head; rotting-wood species have teeth on jaws. Range: most of US and Canada. Habitat: wooded, damp areas, in wood or soil. Undesirable.

11 HONEY BEE *(Apis mellifera)*, ¹/₄–³/₄ inch, brown to black with yellow to orange bands, translucent wings. Range: US; all but northernmost Canada. Habitat: open grassy and wooded areas. How to attract: flowers for nectar.

12 BALD-FACED HORNET
(Vespula maculata), ¹/₂–³/₄ inch, black with distinct yellow to white lines on head, thorax, and abdomen. Range: all US and Canada. Habitat: lawns, gardens, weedy areas, and woodlands. Will sting repeatedly with little provocation.

13 GALL WASP *(Family Cynipidae)*, ¹/₈–¹/₄ inch, brown to red-brown, flattened on sides, yellowish wings. Range: all US; southern Canada. Habitat: wooded areas and parks. How to attract: tree and weed species preferred as gall sites.

14 BLACK CARPENTER ANT
(Camponotus pennsylvanicus), ¹/₄–¹/₂ inch, black, red-brown where legs and segments join. Range: eastern US and southeastern Canada, west to North Dakota. Habitat: dead wood. Can be a damaging pest.

15 BRACONID WASP *(Apanteles* spp.)*, ¹/₁₆–¹/₈ inch, black with yellow areas on legs, clear wings lightly veined. Range: all US and Canada. Habitat: open areas, and gardens. How to attract: nectar plants for adults. Beneficial pest-eater.

1 CRANE FLY *(Tipula* spp.), $^3/_8$–2$^1/_2$ inches, gray to brown, legs longer than body. Range: all US and Canada. Habitat: generally near water. How to attract: water.

2 DRAGONFLY *(Order Odonata)*, $^3/_4$–4$^1/_2$ inches, many colors, often brilliant, large eyes, four slender wings. Range: all US and Canada. Habitat: near water.

3 JUNE BEETLE *(Phyllophaga* spp.), $^3/_4$–1$^3/_8$ inches, red-brown to black, well-developed hindwings. Range: all US and Canada. Habitat: grassy areas, wooded areas.

4 AMERICAN CARRION BEETLE *(Silpha americana)*, $^5/_8$–$^7/_8$ inch, yellowish pronotum, brown elytra with raised edges, black head. Range: US and southern Canada, west to Rockies. Habitat: very widespread, wherever carrion is found.

5 BLACK BLISTER BEETLE *(Epicauta lemniscata)*, $^1/_2$–$^5/_8$ inch, black, hairs along elytra, bulging head. Range: eastern US. Habitat: grassy, weedy areas.

6 TWO-SPOTTED LADY BEETLE *(Adalia bipunctata)*, $^1/_8$–$^1/_4$ inch, black head and thorax, orange elytra with two black spots. Range: all US and Canada. Habitat: grassy, weedy areas.

7 POMACE FLY *(Drosophila melanogaster)*, $^1/_{16}$–$^1/_8$ inch, yellowish with brown bands on abdomen, red eyes. Range: all US and Canada. Habitat: near water or damp areas.

8 JAPANESE BEETLE *(Popillia japonica)*, $^3/_8$–$^1/_2$ inch, shimmering green body, red-brown elytra. Range: eastern US. Habitat: weedy areas, wooded areas.

9 DEER FLY *(Chrysops* spp.), $^3/_8$–$^5/_8$ inch, black with green on thorax and abdomen, bright green eyes, tinted wings. Range: all US and Canada. Habitat: woodlands and backyards.

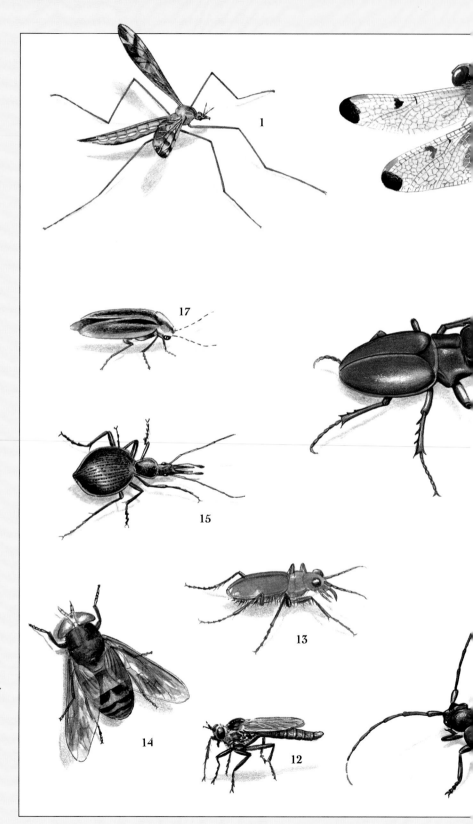

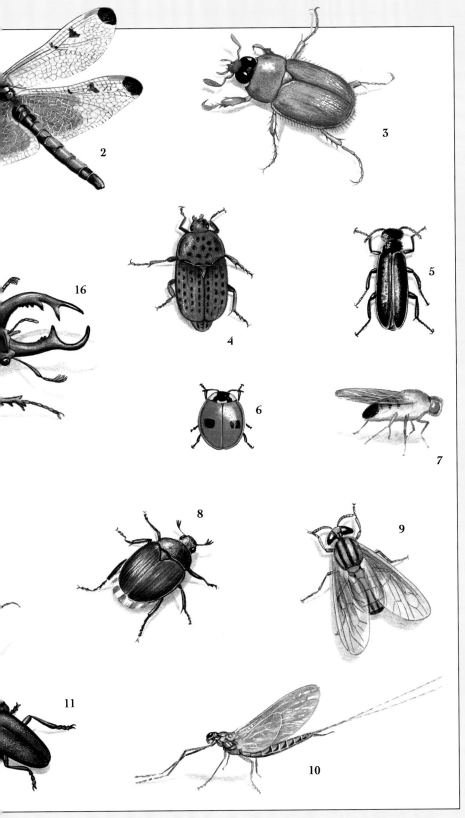

10 MAYFLY (Order *Ephemeroptera*), 1/4–7/8 inch, brown to yellow, filament-like tails. Range: all US and Canada. Habitat: near clean water.

11 BRASSY METALLIC WOOD BORER (*Dicerca divaricata*), 1/8–3/4 inch, dark brown with brassy spotting. Range: all US; southernmost Canada. Habitat: woody, brushy areas.

12 COMMON GRAY ROBBER FLY (*Tolomeus notatus*), 1/2–1 inch, gray to dull black, protruding eyes, veined wings. Range: all US and Canada. Habitat: wooded and adjacent areas.

13 SIX-SPOTTED TIGER BEETLE (*Cicindela sexguttata*), 1/2–5/8 inch, shimmering green to blue-green, white spots at elytra rear. Range: eastern US; Canada. Habitat: wooded areas and clearings.

14 BLACK HORSE FLY (*Tabanus atratus*), 3/4–1 1/8 inches, black with off-white hair on thorax, tinted wings. Range: most of US and southern Canada. Habitat: weedy areas.

15 COMMON BLACK GROUND BEETLE (*Pterostichus* spp.), 1/2–5/8 inch, shimmering black, red-brown legs and antennae. Range: all US and Canada. Habitat: gardens, fields.

16 GIANT STAG BEETLE (*Lucanus elaphus*), 1 1/8–2 3/8 inches, red-brown, darker legs and antennae; male has antlerlike jaws. Range: eastern US. Habitat: wooded areas.

17 PENNSYLVANIA FIREFLY (*Photuris pennsylvanicus*), 3/8–5/8 inch, reddish head with black center spot, gray-brown edged yellow elytra. Range: eastern US and Canada. Habitat: grassy, weedy areas.

1 GRAPEVINE LEAFHOPPER
(Erythroneura comes), ¹⁄₁₆–¹⁄₈ inch, yellowish with bright red and blue markings, three black dots on each forewing. Range: all US and Canada. Habitat: weedy areas, grassy areas, gardens. How to attract: grape vines, beech, maple, plum.

2 BROADWINGED KATYDID
(Microcentrum rhombifolium), 2–2¹⁄₂ inches, dark green, forewings at least three times as long as wide. Range: all but southernmost US. Habitat: wooded areas, meadows. How to attract: no special efforts.

3 BUSH KATYDID *(Scudderia furcata)*, 1⁵⁄₈–2 inches, green with long, slender wings. Range: all US; all but northernmost Canada. Habitat: wooded areas. Can be a pest species, especially to fruit trees and shrubs.

4 PERIODICAL CICADA
(Magicicada septendecim), 1–1¹⁄₄ inches, brown-black, bulging wine-red eyes, red legs, wings tinted orange. Range: eastern US. Habitat: wooded areas, adjacent grassy or weedy areas. A pest species, potentially harmful to roots of trees.

5 SNOWY TREE CRICKET
(Oecanthus fultoni), ¹⁄₂–⁵⁄₈ inch, light green, black spots on antennae, transparent wings. Range: all but southernmost US; Canada. Habitat: wooded areas. Adult can be a beneficial insect, eating aphids and caterpillars.

6 NORTHERN MOLE CRICKET *(Gryllotalpa hexadactyla)*, ³⁄₄–1³⁄₈ inches, dull brown, fine hair, broad forelegs. Range: US and southern Canada, west to the Rockies. Habitat: moist soil. Can be a garden pest species.

7 AMERICAN GRASSHOPPER
(Schistocerca americana), 1¹⁄₂–2¹⁄₄ inches, brown to green with cream stripes and black dots along sides, red-brown legs. Range: US and southern Canada, from Appalachian Mountains west to Rockies. Habitat: grassy areas.

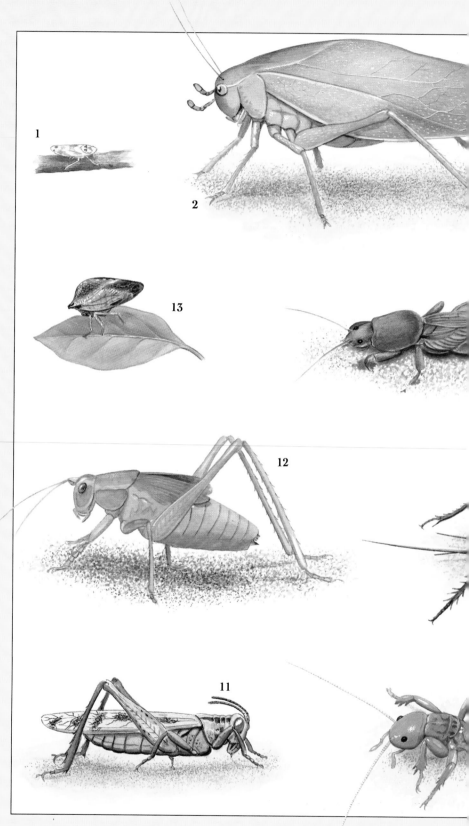

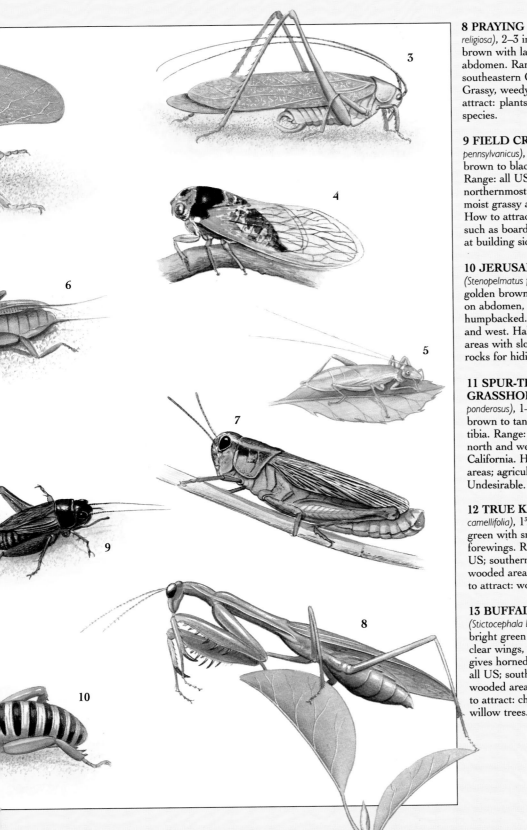

8 PRAYING MANTIS (*Mantis religiosa*), 2–3 inches, green to green-brown with large wings covering abdomen. Range: eastern US; southeastern Canada. Habitat: Grassy, weedy areas. How to attract: plants that attract prey species.

9 FIELD CRICKET (*Gryllus pennsylvanicus*), ½–1 inch, dark brown to black, long antennae. Range: all US; all but northernmost Canada. Habitat: moist grassy and weedy areas. How to attract: covered areas, such as boards on ground or grass at building sides.

10 JERUSALEM CRICKET (*Stenopelmatus fuscus*), 1⅛–2 inches, golden brown with darker bands on abdomen, no wings, large head, humpbacked. Range: US - Nebraska and west. Habitat: grassy, weedy areas with slopes and plenty of rocks for hiding.

11 SPUR-THROATED GRASSHOPPER (*Melanoplus ponderosus*), 1–1½ inches, yellow-brown to tan with red-tinted rear tibia. Range: southeastern US, north and west to Alaska and California. Habitat: Grassy, weedy areas; agricultural areas. Undesirable.

12 TRUE KATYDID (*Pterophylla camellifolia*), 1¾–2¼ inches, bright green with small but heavily veined forewings. Range: eastern half of US; southern Canada. Habitat: wooded areas, shrubby areas. How to attract: wooded areas.

13 BUFFALO TREEHOPPER (*Stictocephala bisonia*), ¼–⅜ inch, bright green above, yellow below, clear wings, protruding pronotum gives horned appearance. Range: all US; southern Canada. Habitat: wooded areas, weedy areas. How to attract: cherry, elm, locust, or willow trees.

1 TIGER SWALLOWTAIL
(*Pterourus glaucus*), 3–5½ inches,
yellow with black tiger stripes from
wider in front to more narrow
toward back. Range: eastern US;
and southeastern Canada northwest to Alaska. Habitat: wooded
areas, gardens. How to attract:
butterfly bush, honeysuckle,
bee balm.

2 RED ADMIRAL
(*Vanessa atalanta*), 1¾–2¼ inches,
black with circular band of orange
through middle of forewing and
outer edge of hindwing. Range: all
US; all but northernmost Canada.
Habitat: woodland edges. How to
attract: nettles.

3 GIANT SWALLOWTAIL
(*Heraclides cresphontes*), 3½–5½
inches, black with bands of light
yellow patches straight across
wings and another along rim.
Range: eastern US and
southeastern Canada, west to the
Rockies. Habitat: open and
wooded areas. How to attract:
citrus trees, goldenrod, lantana.

4 WHITE ADMIRAL (*Basilarchia
arthemis*), ¾–3¼ inches, black with
U-shaped band of white patches
along wings and band of orange
patches outside white. Range:
northeastern US; southeastern
Canada. Habitat: open, wooded
areas. How to attract: birches,
willows.

5 ZEBRA SWALLOWTAIL
(*Eurytides marcellus*), 2¼–3½ inches,
white to pale blue-green with black
stripes front to back. Range:
eastern US. Habitat: wooded areas
near water. How to attract:
pawpaws and related species.

6 VICEROY (*Basilarchia archippus*),
2½–3 inches, orange with a black
postmedian line and distinct black
veins, white patches along black
margins. Range: all but West Coast
of US and southern Canada.
Habitat: moist areas. How to
attract: willows, poplars, fruit trees.

7 MONARCH (*Danaus plexippus*), 3¼–4 inches, orange with distinct black veins and black border flecked with small white and orange patches. Range: all but northwest US; southern Canada. Habitat: diverse. How to attract: milkweed.

8 SPICEBUSH SWALLOWTAIL (*Pterourus troilus*), 3½–4½ inches, black with band of white patches along margin and chalky blue band along hindwings. Range: eastern US; southeastern Canada. Habitat: wooded areas, meadows, gardens. How to attract: spicebush, milkweed, clover.

9 PIPEVINE SWALLOWTAIL (*Battus philenor*), 2¾–3½ inches, black forewings, duller at margins; chalky blue and black hindwings. Range: all but northwest US; southern Canada. Habitat: open areas. How to attract: pipevines, honeysuckle, milkweed.

10 RED-SPOTTED PURPLE (*Basilarchia astyanax*), 3–3½ inches, black with purple shading, submarginal blue bars. Range: US and Canada, west to the Rockies. Habitat: open woods and grass. How to attract: hawthorns, willows, poplars, cherries, apples.

11 CLODIUS PARNASSIAN (*Parnassius clodius*), 2¼–3 inches, white to gray-white with a few scattered red to orange spots. Range: northwestern US; southwestern Canada. Habitat: wooded areas at higher elevations. How to attract: bleeding heart and other *Dicentra* spp.

12 EASTERN BLACK SWALLOWTAIL (*Papilio polyxenes*), 2¾–3½ inches, black with double band of yellow patches. Range: eastern US and southeastern Canada, west to the Rockies. Habitat: grassy, weedy areas. How to attract: plants in the carrot family.

1 CHALCEDON CHECKERSPOT (*Occidryas chalcedona*), 1¼–2 inches, completely banded in patches of orange, cream, and black with distinct black lines between patches and bands. Range: southwestern US. Habitat: dry, open areas. How to attract: plantain, honeysuckle, figwort.

2 MOURNING CLOAK (*Nymphalis antiopa*), 2¾–3¼ inches, black with submarginal band of blue patches and marginal band of cream-yellow. Range: all US; all but northernmost Canada. Habitat: wooded areas with openings. How to attract: Shasta daisy, butterfly bush, milkweed.

3 BUCKEYE (*Junonia coenia*), 2–2½ inches, tan with two patches of orange at costa of forewing, submarginal band of large concentric circles of purple inside cream inside black. Range: US and southern Canada, west to Rockies; and northwestern US. Habitat: open areas.

4 GRAY HAIRSTREAK (*Strymon melinus*), 1–1¼ inches, gray-brown forewings, blue-gray hindwings. Range: all US; southern Canada. Habitat: open areas or open woodlands. How to attract: many different domestic and wildflower species and trees.

5 BALTIMORE (*Euphydryas phaeton*), 1½–2½ inches, black with red-orange patches at wing cells followed by four broken bands of white patches, scalloped band of orange along margins. Range: eastern US, except Deep South; southeastern Canada. Habitat: moist, wooded areas.

6 PAINTED LADY (*Vanessa cardui*), 2–2¼ inches, tan with lateral band of orange, black patches and black tips with white patches. Range: all US; all but northernmost Canada. Habitat: nearly universal. How to attract: many species of wildflowers.

7 LARGE WOOD NYMPH
(Cercyonis pegala), 2–3 inches, brown with two darker, white-centered spots on forewing. Range: US and Canada, excluding southernmost US, northernmost Canada, and West Coast. Habitat: wooded areas; grassy areas. How to attract: various grass species.

8 PEARLY CRESCENTSPOT
(Phyciodes tharos), 1–1½ inches, orange outline, circular patches near body, black-banded; heavy black mottling at apex of forewing. Range: US; all but northernmost Canada west to Rockies. Habitat: damp, open areas. How to attract: aster, thistle.

9 QUESTION MARK *(Polygonia interrogationis)*, 2¼–2¾ inches, orange with scattered black patches and spots, thin purple-blue border. Range: eastern US and southeastern Canada, west to Rockies. Habitat: open, wooded areas. How to attract: aster, nettles, hackberries, sweet pepperbush.

10 AMERICAN PAINTED LADY *(Vanessa virginiensis)*, 1¾–2¼ inches, orange with black jack-o-lantern face on each forewing. Range: all US; all but northernmost Canada. Habitat: open areas. How to attract: composites, zinnia, yarrow, scabiosa, heliotrope.

11 COMMA *(Polygonia comma)*, 1¾–2 inches, orange with sparsely scattered black patches and spots. Range: eastern US; southern half of Canada northwest to Rockies. Habitat: moist, wooded areas; suburbs. How to attract: hops, nettles, butterfly bush, snowy stonecrop.

12 SNOUT BUTTERFLY
(Libytheana bachmanii), 1½–2 inches, orange fading to black and white patches, long, pointed snout. Range: band curving from northeast US through Great Lakes west and down through the Rockies. Habitat: wooded areas. How to attract: hackberry, dogwood.

1 COMMON SULPHUR (*Colias philodice*), 1½–2 inches, pale yellow with black borders and one black dot on each forewing. Range: all US; all but northernmost Canada. Habitat: open grassy and weedy areas. How to attract: legumes, dandelion, goldenrod, clover, tickseed, milkweed.

2 SILVERY BLUE (*Glaucopsyche lygdamus*), ¾–1¼ inches, blue with some silver tinting and a white-and-gray margin. Range: all but southernmost US and northern Canada. Habitat: open areas. How to attract: legumes, lupines, bitter cherry, coneflowers, damp ground.

3 ORANGE SULPHUR (*Colias eurytheme*), 1½–2½ inches, gold to orange with a pinkish tint and black margins. Range: all but northwest US; all but northernmost and West Coast of Canada. Habitat: open areas. How to attract: legumes, clover, tickseed, dandelion, rabbit bush.

4 EASTERN TAILED BLUE (*Everes comyntas*), ¾–1¼ inches, blue with metallic veins and some metallic dusting, single orange spot on hindwing near white tail. Range: all US; southern Canada. Habitat: disturbed areas. How to attract: legumes.

5 CABBAGE WHITE (*Pieris rapae*), 1¼–1¾ inches, white with one black spot, black tip on each forewing. Range: all US; all but northernmost Canada. Habitat: almost universal. Generally considered a pest species that attacks the crucifers.

6 BRONZE COPPER (*Hyllolycaena hyllus*), 1–1¼ inches, orange-brown with bands of black dots, faint zigzag band of orange on hindwing. Range: northeast through central US; southern Canada. Habitat: moist, grassy areas. How to attract: dock, blue flag.

7 REAKIRT'S BLUE *(Hemiargus isola)*, ³/₄–1¹/₄ inches, light blue with dusting of white and black borders. Range: central US north into south-central Canada. Habitat: disturbed, open areas. How to attract: legumes, many different wildflower species.

8 CLOUDLESS GIANT SULPHUR *(Phoebis sennae)*, 2–2³/₄ inches, yellow with scalloped gray to brown along outer margin of forewing. Range: southern US year-round; north to the Great Lakes in summer. Habitat: open areas; shore areas. How to attract: milkweed, firebush, lantana.

9 SPRING AZURE *(Celastrina ladon)*, ³/₄–1¹/₄ inches, blue with black and white to blue margin. Range: all US; all but northernmost Canada. Habitat: wooded areas, open areas near woodlands. How to attract: dogwoods, blueberries.

10 COMMON WHITE *(Pontia protodice)*, 1¹/₄–2 inches, white checkered with black, gray to brown. Range: all but northwest US. Habitat: disturbed areas, such as fields, backyards, and vacant lots. How to attract: crucifers and capers.

11 AMERICAN COPPER *(Lycaena phlaeas)*, ³/₄–1¹/₄ inches, orange with gray-brown border, black patches on forewing, gray-brown with orange border on hindwing. Range: northern US; Canada. Habitat: open and disturbed areas. How to attract: sorrels, dock, yarrow, daisies.

1 SILVER-BORDERED FRITILLARY (*Clossiana selene*), 1¼–2 inches, orange with broken zigzag lines of black and a broken black band along the margins. Caterpillar is brown with black and yellow speckling; yellow spines. Range: northern two-thirds of US; southern half of Canada. Habitat: Bogs, wet meadows. How to attract: violets.

2 REGAL FRITILLARY (*Speyeria idalia*), 2¾–3¾ inches, orange with black zigzag patches near forewing costa; blue-gray with bands of white patches on hind wing. Range: Great Lakes west to Great Plains, north into Canada and south to Kansas. Habitat: moist woodland or grassland. How to attract: violets as host plant; milkweed, thistle as nectar sources.

3 MEADOW FRITILLARY (*Clossiana bellona*), 1¼–2 inches, orange with zigzag bands, spots and patches of black; tip of forewing bulges outward. Caterpillar is black with yellow patches and dull black spines. Range: northern half of US; southern half of Canada. Habitat: damp wooded or weedy areas. How to attract: violets are a preferred host plant.

4 PEARLY EYE (*Enodia portlandia*), 1¾–2 inches, brown with zigzag bands of darker brown, band of darker spots just inside margin. Caterpillar is striped green with red horns. Range: southeastern US. Habitat: wooded areas, always near cane. How to attract: canes as host plants. Males are highly defensive of selected tree trunks in territories.

5 GREAT SPANGLED FRITILLARY (*Speyeria cybele*), 2–3 inches, light orange, brownish at body, zigzag bands of black. Caterpillar is dark brown with black stripes and spines. Range: northern two-thirds of US; southern Canada. Habitat: open woodlands. How to attract: violets as host plant; thistle, dogbane as nectar sources.

6 COMMON CHECKERED SKIPPER *(Pyrgus communis)*, 1–2 inches, color on wings varies but nearly always have a blue, powdery sheen in the center. Caterpillar is tan with darker lines. Range: all US; southern Canada. Habitat: grassy, weedy, and garden areas. How to attract: mallows are one of many weed types that serve as host plant.

7 EYED BROWN *(Satyrodes eurydice)*, 1½–2 inches, brown with bands of concentrically ringed spots of tan, cream, and black on both wings. Caterpillar is green with yellow stripes along sides and red horns. Range: northern US and southern Canada, west to the Rockies. Habitat: moist, open areas. How to attract: sedges as host plants.

8 GULF FRITILLARY *(Agraulis vanillae)*, 2½–3 inches, bright orange with tadpole-like streaks of black throughout, white, black-edged spots on forewing. Caterpillar is blue-black, striped with red; six straight rows of black spines. Range: all US. Habitat: open, grassy areas. How to attract: passion flowers as host plant and nectar source.

9 SILVER-SPOTTED SKIPPER *(Epargyreus clarus)*, 1¾–2½ inches, dull brown with orange patches along middle of forewing. Caterpillar is light green with darker stripes and patches and a brown head. Range: all US; southern Canada. Habitat: open wooded and grassy areas. How to attract: wisteria, beans, locusts as host plants.

10 FIERY SKIPPER *(Hylephila phyleus)*, 1–1½ inches, brown with a dark jagged edge on wings. Caterpillar is beige with three darker stripes. Range: southern half of US, although more common in east. Habitat: gardens, lawns, and grasslands. How to attract: many different types of native grasses serve as host plants.

1 CECROPIA MOTH (*Hyalophora cecropia*), 5–6 inches, red-brown, white and black spots, red bands. Range: eastern US and southern Canada, west to the Rockies. Habitat: open areas. How to attract: birch, maple, ash, willow, elm, apple, lilac, cherry trees.

2 ISABELLA TIGER MOTH (*Isia isabella*), 1½–2 inches, brown to yellow-brown with black dots; better known for caterpillar, banded woolybear. Range: all US; all but northernmost Canada. Habitat: weedy, grassy areas. How to attract: no special effort needed.

3 IMPERIAL MOTH (*Eacles imperialis*), 4–6 inches, yellow with blue-gray spots and darker specklings. Range: eastern US and southern Canada, west to the Rockies. Habitat: wooded areas. How to attract: wide range of tree foliage is food for caterpillar.

4 TOMATO HORNWORM MOTH (*Manduca quinquemaculata*), 3½–4½ inches, brown-gray with black streaks; heavy body, large eyes. Range: eastern half of US; southeastern Canada. Habitat: open, disturbed areas. Generally considered a pest species.

5 CORN EARWORM (*Helicoverpa zea*), 1–1¾ inches, red-brown with darker spots and stripes. Range: all US; all but northernmost Canada. Habitat: agricultural areas. Generally considered a serious pest species.

6 AMERICAN TENT CATERPILLAR (*Malacosoma americanuai*), 1–1¾ inches, dark brown with two thin white lines on forewing. Range: eastern US; Canada. Habitat: wooded areas. Generally considered a major pest species.

7 PROMETHEA MOTH (*Callosamia promethea*), 3¾–4½ inches, black with tan-gray margins, blue eyespot near apex of forewing. Range: eastern US. Habitat: open areas. How to attract: cherry, sassafras, lilac, sycamore, tulip tree, ash, and other tree species.

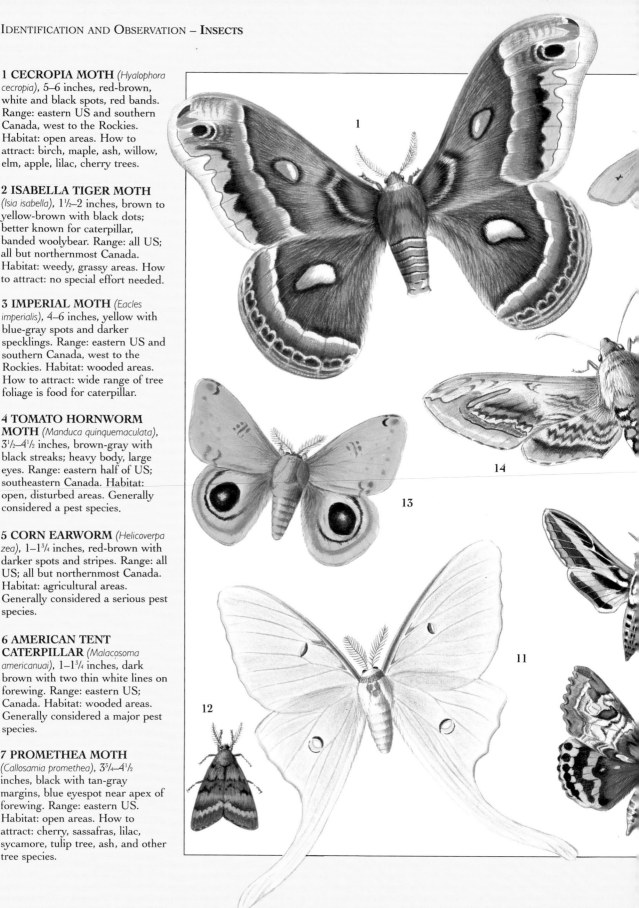

8 POLYPHEMUS MOTH *(Antheraea polyphemus)*, 5–6 inches, tan to gray-brown or green-brown forewing with yellow-ringed transparent eyespot, similar hindwing but with blue eyespot. Range: eastern US. Habitat: open areas. How to attract: oak, elm, birch, maple.

9 CLOUDED LOCUST UNDERWING *(Eupartheus nubilus)*, 2¼–2¾ inches, gray-brown and white in a mottled pattern on forewings, black hindwings with bands of orange-yellow. Range: eastern US; Canada. Habitat: wooded areas. How to attract: black locust.

10 WHITE-LINED SPHINX MOTH *(Hyles lineata)*, 2½–3½ inches, brown forewing with white veins, pinkish hindwing brown at margins, brown abdomen with white stripes. Range: all US; southern Canada. Habitat: grassy, weedy areas. How to attract: portulaca.

11 LUNA MOTH *(Actias luna)*, 3–4½ inches, pale green with purplish band along front and one bright eyespot on each wing. Range: eastern US; southeastern Canada. Habitat: wooded areas. How to attract: birch, walnut, persimmon, and hickory.

12 GYPSY MOTH *(Lymantria dispar)*, ¾–2¾ inches, male – gray-brown with brown lines; female – cream-white with tan lines and brown spots. Range: eastern US; southeastern Canada. Habitat: wooded areas. Generally considered a major forest pest species.

13 IO MOTH *(Automeris io)*, 2⅓–3¼ inches, male – yellow and red hindwings with large eyespot in center, yellow forewings; female – purple forewings. Range: eastern US and southern Canada, west to the Rockies. Habitat: wooded, shrubby areas. How to attract: cherry, elm, apple oak, willow, corn.

1 JUMPING LYNX SPIDER
(Oxyopes spp.), ⅛–⅜ inch, yellow cephalothorax with pale stripes, gray abdomen with iridescent spots, yellow legs with black line on each. Range: all US; southern and central Canada. Habitat: grassy, weedy areas. How to attract: unmowed areas.

2 GARDEN SPIDER *(Araneus diadematus)*, ¼–¾ inch, burnt orange with darker, brown-banded legs, row of diamond-shaped silver spots along abdomen. Range: northeastern US; southeastern Canada. Habitat: gardens, backyards. How to attract: unmowed areas.

3 COMMON HOUSE CENTIPEDE *(Scutigera coleoptrata)*, 1–2½ inches, red-brown, flat segmented body, one pair of long legs from each segment. Range: eastern half of US; southeastern Canada. Habitat: all sheltered locations. Generally considered a pest species.

4 BROWN DADDY-LONG-LEGS *(Phalangium opilio)*, ⅛–⅜ inch, red-brown body, long, thin, dark brown legs. Range: all US; all but northernmost Canada. Habitat: grassy, weedy areas. How to attract: unmowed areas.

5 WOLF SPIDER *(Family Lycosidae)*, ⅛–1⅜ inches, mottled browns and blacks, hairy, eight black eyes in three rows, roundish abdomen and cephalothorax. Range: all US; all but northernmost Canada. Habitat: grassy, weedy areas. How to attract: smaller insect prey.

6 GOLDENROD SPIDER
(Misumena vatia), ⅛–⅜ inch, female – yellow to white with red streaks on sides of abdomen; male – red-brown with white spot in center of cephalothorax and at eyes. Range: all US; southern Canada. Habitat: grassy, weedy areas. How to attract: goldenrod, daisies.

7 EARTHWORM (*Lumbricus terrestris*), to 11 inches, pinkish brown to brown, shimmering. Range: all US; all but northern Canada. Habitat: varies widely. How to attract: discontinue use of all nonorganic additives in the garden.

8 BLACK-AND-YELLOW ARGIOPE (*Argiope aurantia*), ¼–1⅛ inches, black abdomen marked with yellow or orange, silver hair on cephalothorax, black legs with yellow bands. Range: all US; southern Canada. Habitat: grassy, weedy, shrubby areas. How to attract: small shrubs.

9 DARING JUMPING SPIDER (*Phidippus audax*), ¼–¾ inch, black with white band on abdomen; scattered gray spots. Range: eastern US and southern Canada, west to the Rockies. Habitat: wooded areas. How to attract: tree trunks are crucial habitat feature.

10 SIX-SPOTTED ORB WEAVER (*Araniella displicata*), ⅛–⅜ inch, brownish yellow with round black spots on sides. Range: most of US and Canada. Habitat: weedy areas. How to attract: unmowed areas.

11 BANDED MILLIPEDE (*Narceus americanus*), 1–3 inches, purplish to dark gray segments with red bands between, each segment has own pair of legs. Range: all US; southern Canada. Habitat: damp areas with plant litter. How to attract: plant litter in undisturbed location.

12 GRASS SPIDER (*Agelenopsis* spp.), ½–¾ inches, yellow-banded cephalothorax, gray abdomen with darker bands, eyes in two arched lines. Range: all US; all but northernmost Canada. Habitat: grassy, weedy, shrubby areas. How to attract: unmowed areas.

1 PLAINS SPADEFOOT
(*Scaphiopus bombifrons*), 1½–2 inches, gray to brown-gray, darker markings, yellowish or reddish tubercles. Range: central US and Canada. Habitat: open, relatively dry grasslands. How to attract: insects for food.

2 RED EFT (*Notophthalmus viridescens*) (terrestrial form of the aquatic eastern newt), 1¼–5½ inches, bright orange with red, black-encircled spots along sides. Range: eastern half of US; southeastern Canada. Habitat: wooded areas near water. How to attract: habitat.

3 EASTERN SPADEFOOT
(*Scaphiopus holbrookii holbrooki*), 1¾–2¼ inches, brownish with two yellow lines running from eyes along back. Range: eastern US; west to Arkansas. Habitat: wooded areas with sandy, loose soil. How to attract: habitat, insects for food.

4 AMERICAN TOAD (*Bufo americanus*), 2–4½ inches, brown, covered with "warts". Range: eastern US, southeastern Canada. Habitat: moist areas with daytime-hiding cover. How to attract: habitat, insects for food.

5 SPOTTED SALAMANDER
(*Ambystoma maculatum*), 6–10 inches, black to dark brown with two rows of orange spots along back. Range: eastern US; southeastern Canada. Habitat: open forests near water. How to attract: moist leaf litter.

6 LONG-TAILED SALAMANDER (*Eurycea longicauda longicauda*), 4–6¼ inches, yellowish to orange-red with vertical black markings on tail. Range: eastern US. Habitat: rocky areas near water. How to attract: habitat.

7 TIGER SALAMANDER
(*Ambystoma tigrinum*), 5¾–13½ inches, brown-green with cream and black spots, or tiger-striped. Range: East Coast and central US; southcentral Canada. Habitat: damp areas. How to attract: moist leaf litter.

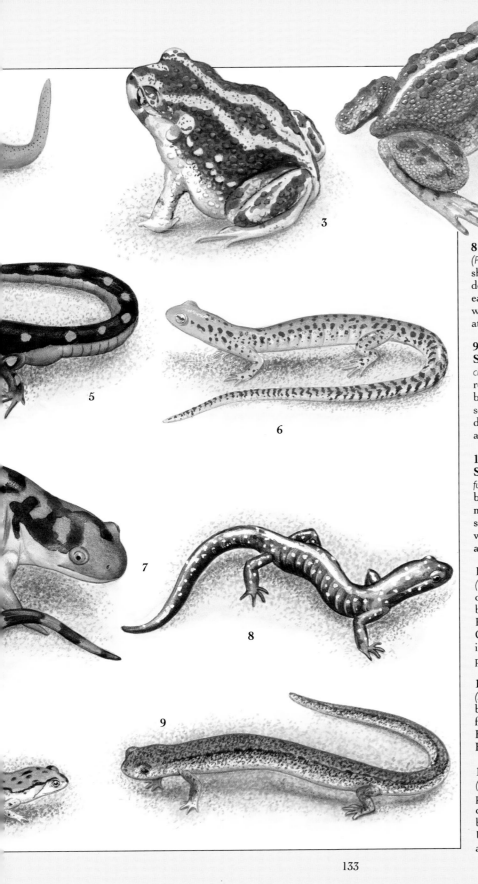

8 SLIMY SALAMANDER
(Plethodon glutinosus), 4–7¼ inches,
shiny black with yellow to cream
dots scattered across body. Range:
eastern US. Habitat: damp,
wooded, and rocky areas. How to
attract: habitat.

9 RED-BACKED
SALAMANDER (Plethodon
cinereus), 2¼–5¼ inches, gray with
red, black-bordered band along
back. Range: northeastern US;
southeastern Canada. Habitat:
damp, wooded areas. How to
attract: habitat.

10 NORTHERN DUSKY
SALAMANDER (Desmognathus
fuscus fuscus), 2½–4½ inches, gray or
brown with slightly darker
markings. Range: eastern US;
southeastern Canada. Habitat:
wooded areas near water. How to
attract: habitat.

11 GREAT PLAINS TOAD
(Bufo cognatus), 1¾–3½ inches, gray
or gray-brown with large dark
blotches bordered by lighter areas.
Range: Great Plains of US and
Canada, west to the Rockies and,
in the south, to California. Habitat:
prairie and desert areas.

12 MOLE SALAMANDER
(Ambystoma talpoideum), 3–4 inches,
black to brown with blue-white
flecks. Range: southeastern US.
Habitat: damp, wooded areas.
How to attract: moist leaf litter.

13 WESTERN GREEN TOAD
(Bufo debilis isidior), 1¼–2¼ inches,
pale green with round black dots
on dorsum, many connected by
black lines. Range: southwestern
US. Habitat: prairie and desert
areas at higher elevations.

1 CHORUS FROG (*Pseudacris triseriata*), ³/₄–1¹/₂ inches, brown, green, or gray with dark stripes along back and dark patches on legs. Range: central US and Canada. Habitat: grassy and wooded areas near water. How to attract: habitat.

2 WOOD FROG (*Rana sylvatica*), 1¹/₄–3¹/₄ inches, tan to brown with dark brown or black mask. Range: eastern US; eastern Canada, west and north to West Coast and to Alaska. Habitat: moist woodlands and grasslands. How to attract: habitat.

3 BULLFROG (*Rana catesbeiana*), 3¹/₂–8 inches, brown-green to yellow-green with mottling and scattered spots of brown or gray. Range: eastern US, west to Great Plains and West Coast; southeastern Canada. Habitat: ponds, lakes, streams, and rivers with underwater vegetation and mud. How to attract: habitat.

4 SPOTTED FROG (*Rana pretiosa*), 2–4 inches, brown with scattered dark spots and dark mask. Range: northwestern US; southwestern Canada. Habitat: near freshwater in mountains, wandering farther afield in spring and summer. How to attract: habitat.

5 NORTHERN CRICKET FROG (*Acris crepitans*), ¹/₂–1¹/₂ inches, mottled tan and green with spots of yellow, red, and black, dark brown bands across legs. Range: East Coast and central US. Habitat: grassy, weedy areas near water. How to attract: Water with surrounding vegetation is critical habitat factor.

6 SOUTHERN CRICKET FROG (*Acris gryllus*), ¹/₂–1¹/₄ inches, mottled black, brown and green with dark triangular spot between eyes. Range: southeastern US. Habitat: edges of damp, swampy places, ranging from lakes and marshes to roadside ditches. How to attract: water with surrounding damp, weedy areas.

7 GREEN FROG (*Rana clamitans*), 2–4¼ inches, green to brown with black spots along back and on legs, bright green nose and lips. Range: eastern US; southeastern Canada. Habitat: ponds, lakes, swamps with plenty of submerged vegetation. How to attract: habitat.

8 PACIFIC TREEFROG (*Hyla regilla*), ¾–2 inches, green to dark brown with dark spots and a black stripe through each eye. Range: West Coast US; southwesternmost Canada. Habitat: grassy, weedy, shrubby areas near water. How to attract: habitat.

9 SPRING PEEPER (*Hyla crucifer*), ¾–1½ inches, shades of brown and gray with a dark X across back. Range: eastern US; southeastern Canada. Habitat: wooded areas directly in water or very close to water. How to attract: habitat.

10 NORTHERN LEOPARD FROG (*Rana pipiens*), 2–5 inches, brown or green with dark, light-bordered spots. Range: all of northern US and southern Canada, except West Coast. Habitat: generally near water, but ranges from freshwater sites to desert and mountain meadows. How to attract: habitat.

11 PICKEREL FROG (*Rana palustris*), 1½–3½ inches, yellowish tan to tan with rows of green-brown to bronze patches and spots running front to back. Range: northeastern US and southeastern Canada, south along the East Coast and southwest through the Great Lakes to Texas. Habitat: moist, weedy areas. How to attract: habitat.

12 RED-LEGGED FROG (*Rana aurora*), 2–5⅜ inches, red-brown to gray with scattered dark spots and a dark mask. Range: West Coast of US; to northwesternmost Canada. Habitat: near heavily vegetated ponds, lakes or swamps. How to attract: habitat.

1 FIVE-LINED SKINK

(*Eumeces fasciatus*), 5–8 inches, brown to black with five yellowish stripes running head to tail. Range: eastern US. Habitat: damp, wooded areas. How to attract: habitat with rotting logs and other plant litter.

2 EASTERN HOGNOSE SNAKE (*Heterodon platyrhinos*),

18–46 inches, brown, gray, yellow, or red with large patches or bands of darker shades. Range: eastern US. Habitat: open grassy or weedy areas with loose, sandy soil. Not easily attracted.

3 COMMON GARTER SNAKE

(*Thamnophis sirtalis*), 16–53 inches, shades of green with lighter stripes along sides and back. Range: most of US and southern Canada, except dry areas of the Southwest. Habitat: moist areas near water. How to attract: habitat.

4 EASTERN BOX TURTLE

(*Terrapene carolina*), 4–10 inches, shell is brown-green with yellow to orange patches, dots, and lines across each segment. Head, neck, legs, and tail are brown to green with yellow markings. Range: US, west to Great Plains. Habitat: moist areas with cover. How to attract: habitat.

5 NORTHERN WATER SNAKE

(*Nerodia sipedon*), 22–56 inches, brown to dark gray either uniformly colored or with darker patches. Range: eastern US; southeasternmost Canada. Habitat: varied, but always near water. Often considered an undesirable species, quick to strike.

6 WOOD TURTLE (*Clemmys insculpta*), 5–9 inches, shell is

brown, very rough; head, neck, legs, and tail are reddish. Range: northeastern US. Habitat: always near water or wetland areas, often in wooded areas. How to attract: habitat, healthy earthworm population.

7 EASTERN FENCE LIZARD
(*Sceloporus undulatus*), 3¹⁄₂–7 inches,
shades of brown, gray, and green;
very heavily scaled. Range:
southern US, west as far as New
Mexico. Habitat: open wooded or
grassy areas. How to attract:
habitat, with ample sunning areas.

8 SHORT-HORNED LIZARD
(*Phrynosoma douglassi*), 2¹⁄₂–6 inches,
gray to yellow- or red-brown, two
rows of darker spots along back;
flat body; hornlike spines on head.
Range: western half US;
southernmost Canada. Habitat:
varies widely, plains to forested
mountains.

9 RINGNECK SNAKE
(*Diadophis punctatus*), 9–30 inches,
dark gray to black with one red,
orange, or yellow band around
neck. Range: eastern and West
Coast US; southeastern Canada.
Habitat: moist wooded or grassy
areas. How to attract: habitat.

1 CHIPPING SPARROW
(*Spizella passerina*), 5–5¾ inches, gray, brown, and black streaks, brown crown, white eyebrow. Range: all but northernmost Canada. Habitat: wooded, residential areas. How to attract: cracked corn.

2 WHITE-THROATED
SPARROW (*Zonotrichia albicollis*), 6–7 inches, streaked brown and black above, gray below, white throat. Range: eastern and West Coast US; northern and eastern Canada. Habitat: wooded areas. How to attract: cracked corn.

3 BLACK-CAPPED
CHICKADEE (*Parus atricapillus*), 4¾–5¾ inches, gray, white underparts, black cap and throat, white cheeks. Range: northern US; all but northernmost Canada. Habitat: wooded areas. How to attract: oil-type sunflower seeds.

4 CAROLINA CHICKADEE
(*Parus carolinensis*), 4–5 inches, similar to black-capped chickadee, but wing feathers show less white when folded. Range: southeastern US. Habitat: wooded areas. How to attract: oil-type sunflower seeds.

5 HOUSE WREN (*Troglodytes
aedon*), 4½–5¼ inches, dusky brown above, paler below. Range: all US; southern Canada. Habitat: residential, agricultural, and wooded areas. How to attract: insects; not a feeder bird.

6 PURPLE FINCH (*Carpodacus
purpureus*), 5½–6½ inches, male – deep red blended with brown streaks; female – streaked brown. Range: all but central and Rockies portions of US and Canada. Habitat: residential and wooded areas. How to attract: sunflower seeds.

7 AMERICAN GOLDFINCH
(*Carduelis tristis*), 4½–5½ inches, male (spring, summer) – bright yellow, black forehead, wings and tail; female, male (winter) – yellow-tinted gray or brown. Range: most of US; southern Canada. Habitat: residential, grasslands. How to attract: niger seeds.

8 SONG SPARROW (*Melospiza melodia*), 5–7 inches, brown and black streaked above, brown and gray head, gray and black below. Range: all but northernmost Canada. Habitat: residential and agricultural areas. How to attract: black-striped sunflower seeds.

9 FOX SPARROW (*Passerella iliaca*), 6½–7½ inches, striped gray-brown, white, and black above, white below with brown spots. Range: all but central part of continent. Habitat: wooded, thicket areas. How to attract: black-striped sunflower seeds.

10 HOUSE FINCH (*Carpodacus mexicanus*), 5–6 inches, male – streaked brown, red forehead and breast; female – streaked brown. Range: all but central and Gulf Coast US; southern Canada. Habitat: residential areas. How to attract: niger seeds.

11 HOUSE SPARROW (*Passer domesticus*), 5–6½ inches, male – black throat, white cheeks, brown nape, gray crown; female – duller. Range: all but northernmost Canada. Habitat: residential and agricultural areas. How to attract: niger seeds, cracked corn.

12 TREE SPARROW (*Spizella arborea*), 5½–6½ inches, gray, streaked brown above, black breast spot, white wing bars. Range: all but southern and West Coast US; northern Canada. Habitat: wooded areas. How to attract: black-striped sunflower seeds.

13 WHITE-CROWNED SPARROW (*Zonotrichia leucophrys*), 6–7½ inches, streaked brown and black above, gray below, striped black and white crown. Range: southern and western US; northern Canada. Habitat: bushy areas. How to attract: sunflower seeds.

1 BLUE JAY (*Cyanocitta cristata*), 12 inches, bright blue above with white and black in wings, face, and tail, whitish below. Range: eastern half of US and Canada. Habitat: wooded and residential areas. How to attract: cracked corn, peanuts, sunflower seeds.

2 BUSHTIT (*Psaltriparus minimus*), 3³/₄–4¹/₄ inches, gray back, brown cheeks, gray-white underside. Range: western US; southwestern Canada. Habitat: scrub, chaparral, and wooded areas. How to attract: wild lilac.

3 COMMON CROW (*Corvus brachyrhynchos*), 17–21 inches, black throughout. Range: all US; all but northern Canada. Habitat: wooded, residential, and agricultural areas. How to attract: corn, bread, table scraps, tall trees.

4 TUFTED TITMOUSE (*Parus bicolor*), 5–6 inches, gray above, white below, rust sides; noticeable crest. Range: eastern half of US. Habitat: wooded and residential areas. How to attract: black-striped sunflower seeds, suet.

5 RED-WINGED BLACKBIRD (*Agelaius phoeniceus*), 7–9¹/₂ inches, male – black with red and yellow shoulder patches; female – streaked brown. Range: all US; all but northern Canada. Habitat: meadows and swamps. How to attract: cracked corn, suet.

6 BREWER'S BLACKBIRD (*Euphagus cyanocephalus*), 8–10 inches, male – black with purple-tinted head; female – brownish gray. Range: US east to Great Lakes and Florida; southwestern Canada. Habitat: agricultural areas. How to attract: cracked corn, millet.

7 PINE SISKIN (*Carauelis pinus*), 4¹/₂–5¹/₄ inches, streaked gray, brown, and white, yellow in wings and tail. Range: all US; all but northcentral and northeastern Canada. Habitat: wooded, residential areas. How to attract: millet, sunflower seeds.

8 AMERICAN ROBIN (*Turdus migratorius*), 9–11 inches, dark gray above, orange-red below, black head and tail. Range: all US and Canada. Habitat: nearly all types. How to attract: healthy earthworm population, berry-producing shrubs.

9 BROWN-HEADED COWBIRD (*Molothrus ater*), 6–8 inches, dark gray to black, male has glossy brown-tinted head. Range: all US; southwestern Canada. Habitat: wooded, residential, and agricultural areas. How to attract: table scraps, cracked corn.

10 CEDAR WAXWING (*Bombycilla cedrorum*), 6½–8 inches, olive brown above, olive yellow below, black mask, yellow tip on tail, red tips of secondary wing feathers. Range: all US; southern Canada. Habitat: wooded and residential areas. How to attract: berry and fruit plants.

11 EASTERN PHOEBE (*Sayornis phoebe*), 6¼–7¼ inches, olive green above, buff-gray below. Range: US west to the Rockies; central and southeastern Canada. Habitat: wooded and residential areas. How to attract: berries, juniper.

12 DARK-EYED JUNCO (*Junco hyemalis*), 5½–6½ inches, slate gray to dull black above, gray breast, white abdomen. Range: all US; all but northeastern Canada. Habitat: wooded and residential areas. How to attract: grains, peanut butter, sweet birch.

13 EUROPEAN STARLING (*Sturnus vulgaris*), 7½–8½ inches, black to brown-black with white flecks. Range: all US; all but northern Canada. Habitat: residential and agricultural areas. How to attract: table scraps, cracked corn, sunflower seeds.

14 COMMON GRACKLE (*Quiscalus quiscula*), 11–13½ inches, black with iridescent tint ranging from blue to bronze, bright yellow eyes. Range: US and southern Canada, west to Rockies. Habitat: wooded and residential areas. How to attract: sunflower seeds, scraps.

1 NORTHERN CARDINAL

(*Cardinalis cardinalis*), 8–9 inches, male – bright red, black face, crest; female – buff with red tint on crest, wings; and tail. Range: eastern US. Habitat: wooded, swampy, and residential areas. How to attract: oil-type sunflower seeds.

2 EASTERN KINGBIRD

(*Tyrannus tyrannus*), 8–9 inches, dark gray above, white below, black head, black white-edged tail. Range: all US except West Coast and extreme southwest; central and southern Canada. Habitat: agricultural areas. How to attract: cherry trees.

3 COMMON FLICKER (*Colaptes auratus*), 12–13 inches, brown with black streaks across back, white with black spots and bib below, red patch on crown. Range: all but northern Canada. Habitat: wooded, residential areas. How to attract: black-striped sunflower seeds, suet.

4 CHIMNEY SWIFT (*Chaetura pelagica*), 4¾–5½ inches, brown-gray, lighter head and underside. Range: US and southern Canada, west to Great Plains. Habitat: residential areas. How to attract: lawn with flying insect population.

5 WOOD THRUSH (*Hylocichla mustelina*), 8 inches, tan above, white below with black to brown spots, rust head. Range: eastern US; southeastern Canada. Habitat: wooded, and residential areas. How to attract: cracked corn, berry-producing plants.

6 BARN SWALLOW (*Hirundo rustica*), 5½–8 inches, blue-black above, red-brown below, on throat, and forehead. Range: all but southeastern US; northern Canada. Habitat: open grassy and weedy areas near water. How to attract: flying insect population, body of water.

7 BLACK-CHINNED HUMMINGBIRD (*Archilochus alexandri*), 3¼–3¾ inches, emerald green above, whitish below; male has black throat and cheeks. Range: western US; southwestern Canada. Habitat: chaparrals foothills. How to attract: feeder.

8 RUFOUS-SIDED TOWHEE (*Pipilo erythrophthalmus*), 7–9½ inches, male – black above and head, white below, red-brown along sides; female – brown where male is black. Range: US; southcentral Canada. Habitat: wooded and residential areas. How to attract: cracked corn.

9 PURPLE MARTIN (*Progne subis*), 7–8½ inches, male – dark blue; female – duller blue above, gray below. Range: all US except Rockies; central Canada. Habitat: residential and agricultural areas. How to attract: martin houses.

10 NORTHERN ORIOLE (*Icterus galbula*), 7–8½ inches, male – black head, tail, and wings, orange rump, breast, and shoulder; female – duller. Range: all but southeastern US; southern Canada. Habitat: wooded areas. How to attract: berries, fruit bits.

11 MOCKINGBIRD (*Mimus polyglottos*), 9–11 inches, gray with white wing and tail patches on black. Range: most of US. Habitat: residential and agricultural areas. How to attract: bits of fruit, suet, berry-producing plants.

12 TREE SWALLOW (*Iridoprocne bicolor*), 5–6¼ inches, bright green-blue above, white below, white chin and cheeks. Range: Gulf and East Coast US; all but northern Canada. Habitat: grassy, weedy areas near water. How to attract: flying insect population, water.

13 RUBY-THROATED HUMMINGBIRD (*Archilochus colubris*), 3½ inches, metallic green above, whitish below; male has bright red throat. Range: eastern US; southeastern and central Canada. Habitat: wooded, residential areas. How to attract: hummingbird feeder.

14 EASTERN BLUEBIRD (*Sialia sialis*), 6½–7½ inches, bright sky blue above, red-brown breast, white belly. Range: eastern US; southeastern Canada. Habitat: agricultural areas. How to attract: berry-producing plants, bluebird houses.

1 MOURNING DOVE (*Zenaida macroura*), 12 inches, gray-brown with black spots on wings, cream head and underparts. Range: all US; southcentral and West Coast Canada. Habitat: agricultural and residential areas. How to attract: cracked corn.

2 WHITE-BREASTED NUTHATCH (*Sitta carolinensis*), 5–6 inches, blue-gray above, white face and below, black crown. Range: all but central US; central and north Canada. Habitat: wooded areas. How to attract: nut meats, suet.

3 COOPER'S HAWK (*Accipiter cooperii*), 14–20 inches, slate gray above, buff with rust bars below, round-tipped tail. Range: all but northernmost Canada. Habitat: wooded areas.

4 DOWNY WOODPECKER (*Picoides pubescens*), 6–7 inches, black and white streaked above, gray-white below, male has red patch on nape. Range: all but southwestern US and northeastern Canada. Habitat: wooded and residential areas. How to attract: suet.

5 NORTHERN BOBWHITE (*Colinus virginianus*), 8–11 inches, brown, paler and streaked below, white throat and eyebrow. Range: southeastern US, west and north to Wyoming and Ontario. Habitat: agricultural areas. How to attract: thickets.

6 SHARP-SHINNED HAWK (*Accipiter striatus*), 10–14 inches, slate gray above, buff with rust bars below, square-tipped tail. Range: nearly all North America. Habitat: wooded areas.

7 HAIRY WOODPECKER (*Picoides villosus*), 8½–10½ inches, black with rows of white spots, white back, white below, male has red patch. Range: all but northeastern US. Habitat: wooded areas. How to attract: suet.

8 RED-BELLIED WOODPECKER (*Melanerpes carolinus*), 10 inches, barred white and black above, buff below, red

patch on abdomen, male has red crown and nape. Range: eastern US. Habitat: wooded areas. How to attract: suet, hardwood trees.

9 BARN OWL *(Tyto alba)*, 18 inches, yellowish brown above, white with dark spots below, heart-shaped face. Range: all US; southern Canada. Habitat: agricultural, residential, and wooded areas. How to attract: sheltered nesting spots.

10 RING-NECKED PHEASANT *(Phasianus colchicus)*, 21–36 inches, male – shades of brown, gray and white, white neck ring, scarlet wattles, iridescent head; female – streaked shades of brown. Range: northern US; southern Canada. Habitat: grassy, weedy agricultural area, brush. How to attract: corn.

11 AMERICAN KESTREL *(Falco sparverius)*, 9–12 inches, male – pale blue-gray wings with black spots, rust back and tail, whitish below; female – rust where male is blue-gray. Range: all but northernmost Canada. Habitat: residential, and agricultural areas. How to attract: populations of insects and small birds.

12 SCREECH OWL *(Otus asio)*, 10 inches, mottled red-brown or gray, prominent ear tufts. Range: all US; southern and western Canada. Habitat: wooded, and residential areas. How to attract: cavities for nesting.

13 RED-BREASTED NUTHATCH *(Sitta canadensis)*, 4½–4¾ inches, black cap, white eyebrow, blue-gray above, red-brown below; female paler. Range: all US; all but northern Canada. Habitat: conifers. How to attract: black-striped sunflower seeds.

14 CALIFORNIA QUAIL *(Lophortyx californicus)*, 9½–11 inches, male – brown and gray with black plume on head, red-brown crown, black throat; female – duller. Range: western US; southwestern Canada. Habitat: brushy, agricultural, and chaparral areas. How to attract: peanut butter.

1 GRAY SQUIRREL (*Sciurus carolinensis*), 8–12 inches, tail 8–10 inches, grizzled gray flecked with black and white, white belly and breast, thick bushy tail edged with white. Range: US and southern Canada, west to Great Plains; US west of Rockies. Habitat: deciduous woodlands. How to attract: corn, sunflower seeds, cavities for nesting.

2 RED SQUIRREL (*Tamiasciurus hudsonicus*), 7½–10 inches, tail 3½–7 inches, red to reddish brown with flecks of gray and olive, white underside, often a black side line, bushy tail redder than body. Range: northern US, south along Appalachians and Rockies; all but northern Canada. Habitat: coniferous or mixed forests. How to attract: conifer cones.

3 EASTERN COTTONTAIL (*Sylvilagus floridanus*), 14–18½ inches, tail 1–2¾ inches, mottled gray, brown, black, and white, tan to blue-white underside, white tail. Range: US, west to Great Plains. Habitat: agricultural, wooded, and residential areas. How to attract: habitat, bits of apple placed near cover.

4 EASTERN CHIPMUNK (*Tamias striatus*), 5½–9½ inches, tail 3–4½ inches, orange-brown to

gray-brown with side stripes of black and white, white underside. Range: eastern US, except for Deep South; eastern Canada, north to Hudson Bay. Habitat: wooded, shrubby, and rocky areas. How to **attract:** all types of nuts and seeds.

5 THIRTEEN-LINED GROUND SQUIRREL *(Spermophilus tridecemlineatus)*, 4½–7½ inches, tail 2¼–5 inches, body lined with 13 alternating tan and dark brown stripes, carrying rows of spots. Range: central US; southcentral Canada. Habitat: short-grass areas. Often considered a damaging pest in the backyard.

6 FLYING SQUIRREL *(Glaucomys sabrinus* – northern; *G. volanus* – southern)*, 5½–7 inches, tail 3½–6 inches, gray-tan to reddish tan with black line along side, tail lacks bushy quality. Range: (northern) northern US; southern and central Canada; (southern) eastern half of US. Habitat: mixed woodlands.

7 WOODCHUCK *(Marmota monax)*, 16–30 inches, tail 3½–7 inches, grizzled gray, black, white, and brown, darker on forehead and tail. Range: northeastern and northcentral US; southern and central Canada. Habitat: agricultural and residential areas. Often considered a damaging, tunneling, and crop-eating pest in the backyard.

8 FOX SQUIRREL *(Sciurus niger)*, 11–21 inches, tail 7–13 inches, grizzled brown-gray to olive gray, reddish tan at face, paws, and underside, thick bushy tail edged with red-brown. Range: US and southern Canada, west to Great Plains. Habitat: deciduous woodlands. How to **attract:** corn, sunflower seeds, cavities for nesting.

9 BLACK-TAILED JACKRABBIT *(Lepus californicus)*, 22–26 inches, tail 2½–4½ inches, mottled gray, tan, and white, white ring around each eye and on underside, black-tipped tail and ears. Range: western US. Habitat: grassy areas with thick cover. How to **attract:** habitat.

1 MEADOW VOLE (*Microtus pennsylvanicus*), 5¼–7¾ inches, tail 1¼–2½ inches, brown flecked with black and white above, silver-gray below, darker brown feet and tail. Range: northern US; all but northern Canada. Habitat: grassy, weedy areas. How to attract: unmowed, sheltered corners of backyard.

2 NORWAY RAT (*Rattus norvegicus*), 12½–19¼ inches, tail 4¾–8½ inches, brownish gray to olive above, pale gray below, naked pink ears, tail, and feet. Range: all US; southern Canada. Habitat: always found near human habitation or agricultural areas. Generally considered a pest species.

3 HOUSE MOUSE (*Mus musculus*), 5–7¾ inches, tail 2¼–4 inches, gray-brown, paler on underside, very thinly furred tail. Range: all US; and all but northern Canada. Habitat: always found near human habitation. Generally considered a pest species, destroying food supplies and contributing to spread of disease.

4 MEADOW JUMPING MOUSE (*Zapus hudsonius*), 7–10 inches, tail 4¼–6 inches, brown above with yellowish sides and white below. Range: northeastern US; southern and central Canada. Habitat: moist, agricultural areas. How to attract: unmowed areas of grass and weeds.

5 SHORT-TAILED SHREW (*Blarina brevicauda*), 3½–5½ inches, tail ½–1 inch, dark gray highlighted with silver, short pink snout, pink feet. Range: northeastern US, south along Appalachians; southeastern and southcentral Canada. Habitat: wet, wooded areas. How to attract: habitat.

6 EASTERN MOLE (*Scalopus aquaticus*), 3–9 inches, tail ½–1 inch, gray to brown, very wide, heavily clawed forefeet with palms turned to outside. Range: eastern US, except New England and

Appalachians. Habitat: weedy, grassy areas with loose, dry soil. How to attract: habitat.

7 STAR-NOSED MOLE
(*Condylura cristata*), 4½–5 inches, tail 2–3½ inches, black, 22 pink tentacle-like projections around the nose, large scaly forelegs. Range: northeastern US; southeastern Canada. Habitat: damp, grassy areas with soft soil. How to attract: habitat.

8 DEER MOUSE (*Peromyscus maniculatus*), 4½–8 inches, tail 1¾–4 inches, gray-brown to brown above, white below, pink feet. Range: all but southern US and northern Canada. Habitat: brushy, wooded areas. How to attract: all types of seeds placed on ground near brush or wood piles.

9 POCKET MOUSE (*Perognathus* spp.), 3¾–8¼ inches, tail 1¾–4¾ inches, brown to yellowish brown, paler underside separated by buff side stripe. Range: western US; southwesternmost Canada. Habitat: varied, but generally with loose, sandy soil. How to attract: habitat.

10 MASKED SHREW (*Sorex cinereus*), 1¾–4½ inches, tail 1–2 inches, gray-brown above, silver-gray below, brown pointed snout is heavily whiskered. Range: northern US; all of Canada. Habitat: moist agricultural, residential, and wooded areas. How to attract: habitat.

1 RINGTAIL *(Bassariscus astutus)*, 24–32 inches, tail 12–17 inches, yellowish brown to yellowish gray above, off-white below, 14 to 16 alternating bands of black and white around bushy tail. Range: southwestern US. Habitat: canyons and rocky areas. How to attract: secluded areas of rocks for denning.

2 VIRGINIA OPOSSUM *(Didelphis virginiana)*, 25–42 inches, tail 10–19 inches, grizzled gray, white, and black, noticeably thin hairs, pink to black, pink-tipped ears, naked scaly tail. Range: eastern US, west to Great Plains; southeasternmost Canada. Habitat: wooded, agricultural, and residential areas. How to attract: table scraps.

3 BLACK BEAR *(Ursus americanus)*, 54–84 inches, tail 3–6 inches, 36–54 inches at shoulder, black to cinnamon, sometimes white patch on chest, tan snout, very muscular. Range: (growing) all but southwestern US; all but northern Canada. Habitat: wooded and wetland areas. A very powerful animal that should not be desensitized to humans.

4 WHITE-TAILED DEER *(Odocoileus virginianus)*, 54–72 inches, tail 6–14 inches, 34–48 inches at shoulder, red- to gray-brown above, white below, tail brown above, white below, males and some females have antlers. Range: all but southwestern US; southern Canada. Habitat: wooded and agricultural areas. How to attract: salt blocks, apples.

5 RED FOX (*Vulpes vulpes*), 35–44 inches, tail 13–18 inches, 14–17 inches at shoulder, red to red-brown above, white to buff below, black legs, feet, and ears, bushy tail of same color as body. Range: eastern US, west to Rockies; northwest US; most of Canada. Habitat: wooded and agricultural areas. How to attract: fish heads and table scraps.

6 STRIPED SKUNK (*Mephitis mephitis*), 20–33 inches, tail 7–16 inches, black with two white stripes along back (white pattern varies widely), bushy black tail usually has white edges. Range: most of US; southern and central Canada. Habitat: wooded and agricultural areas. How to attract: *see* spotted skunk.

7 RACCOON (*Procyon lotor*), 23–38 inches, tail 7–16 inches, grizzled gray to gray-brown, five to nine alternating rings of black and gray-to yellow-brown around bushy tail, black mask. Range: most of US; southern Canada. Habitat: wooded, shrubby areas, generally within proximity of water. How to attract: eggs and honey, but caution is advised because raccoons are primary rabies victims.

8 COYOTE (*Canis latrans*), 40–52 inches, tail 11–15 inches, 23–27 inches at shoulders, gray to gray-brown flecked with white and black above, buff below, bushy tail with black tip. Range: (growing) all but southeastern US and northern Canada. Habitat: brushy areas throughout range; plains in the West. Can become a dangerous pest species.

9 SPOTTED SKUNK (*Spilogale putorius*), 13½–23 inches, tail 2¾–9 inches, black with irregular bands of white spots along body, black tail with brushy white tip. Range: central and Deep South US. Habitat: wooded and agricultural areas. How to attract: table scraps but caution advised because of foul-smelling spray and involvement with rabies.

THE NATURAL CHAIN OF LIFE

WHEN YOU INVITE WILDLIFE guests into your backyard, you can expect them to behave like any human guests that you've ever had over. They'll bring all their habits and behaviors – ranging from amusing, cute, and cuddly to shocking, repulsive, and even cruel – with them. Just because they're in a nice, safe, and civilized backyard doesn't mean they've left their natural lifestyles behind them, somewhere out there in the "wild."

In addition to the tender moments of mothers looking after their young and the comical antics of some species, you're going to be witness to some fierce and vicious killings. Some newcomers to the pursuit of wildlife gardening and watching are put off by this.

There is really no justification for such human revulsion. Each species is simply doing what comes quite naturally to it. Life in this real and natural world includes death as a regular and frequent occurrence. All living things in the wild state are part of the chain of life. And in this chain of life every living thing is eventually food for others.

The chain begins with plants, which through photosynthesis use the sun's energy to convert simple inorganic substances into usable food in the form of leaves, stems, barks, flowers, seeds, and fruits. Plant-eaters (herbivores) – from caterpillars to rabbits to elk – feed on this plant-produced food. They, in turn, become food for meat-eating (carnivorous) predators, such as insect-eating birds, foxes, and wolves.

Many animals that we normally consider herbivores will also take to predatory habits when food is easily available. Squirrels, for example, spend most of their year eating nuts, seeds, and other plant parts, but each spring they take a heavy toll on nestling birds.

The predators are sometimes themselves food for larger predators. Also, all levels of predator will die from diseases and – much more rarely than you might imagine – old age. When they do, they become food for scavengers, such as vultures, and for decomposers, such as

ABOVE: Death will eventually come into any fully functioning backyard habitat. Red-tailed hawks have been killing and eating cottontail rabbits for thousands of years.

earthworms, fungi, and bacteria. Again, many species, both herbivores and carnivores, will turn to scavenging when the opportunity presents itself.

The decomposers are the final stage for this cycle of the chain of life. They break all dead things down into their most basic and simple, inorganic compounds, such as water and carbon dioxide. As stated earlier, it is these simple, inorganic compounds that the plants convert into the food that begins the entire chain again.

Throughout this chain there is yet another group, the parasites. These generally small creatures, such as lice, mites, and ticks, live and feed on or in other animals.

As we move through the chain, less of the original energy in the food is available to the animal that is currently doing the eating. This is one of the primary reasons that there are fewer numbers of animals at each level. There are fewer plant-eaters than plants, fewer predators than plant-eaters, and fewer large predators than smaller ones.

The diets of the latter stage animals in the chain also are much less specialized than those in the earlier stages. For example, while a fox will hunt and eat just about any smaller animal that it encounters, most caterpillars are strictly limited to one or a few species of plants.

ABOVE: Conflict is natural in the wildlife world where conditions rarely remain static for very long. Forget the "Disney" image of animals, where all species live in harmony and can talk with one another. Struggle and dominance are important survival factors in the lives of most wild animals, such as these squabbling blue jays.

BELOW: Composting of organic yard and household waste can be done with many devices. Circulation of air at the sides is the most critical consideration.

CREATING MULCH

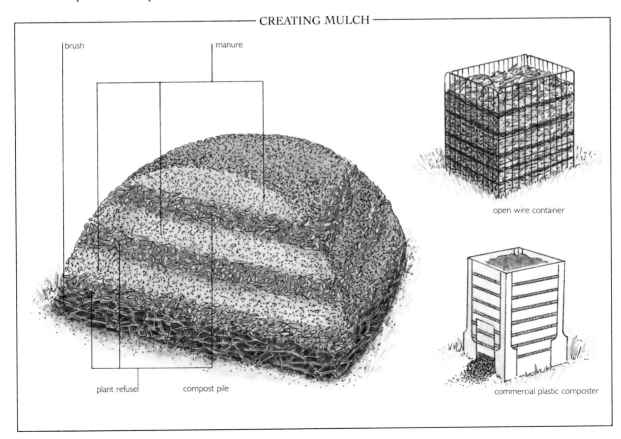

brush

manure

plant refuse

compost pile

open wire container

commercial plastic composter

DEALING WITH PROBLEMS

SOME PEOPLE REALLY DON'T want to be privy to the natural order of life, so they are probably better off outside the realm of backyard habitatting. But even those who understand and accept this situation may want to give the prey species a bit of a helping hand.

Normally, I prefer to let nature run its course. I admire the predators and marvel at their diverse skills in taking their prey. However, in most backyard situations today, humans have added a predator that we must do everything we possibly can to thwart.

The domestic cat, when left to roam free, is an amazingly efficient killer. Much more so than most members of the cat fancy realize or will acknowledge. "Kitty," "Snowball," and "Tabby" have never lost their killer instinct and skill. That in itself is not an unpardonable crime. But most domestic cats are already well-fed and have no true need for the prey they kill. Often it is deposited at the feet of some horrified owner, who simply tosses it in with the trash. For some reason, these same owners never seem to learn to keep their cats inside or restrained when outside.

The plant life that you're already developing in your habitat, particularly thickets, hedgerows, and clusters of thick shrubs, will provide ample escape cover throughout most of the backyard. However, the areas around your feeders and water sources might need special attention. Dense shrubs and brush piles 8 to 10 feet away will foil the attempts of most

ABOVE: Free-roaming domestic cats are extremely dangerous to much of the wildlife that your habitat attracts. The cats represent an unnatural element that really should be prevented if at all possible.

cats. Incidentally, for those who prefer not to have any killing at all in their backyards, this same placement will protect most backyard creatures from hawks and owls.

This same cover will provide perches for subordinate birds, those species that feed and bathe according to a flock-wide pecking order, to await their turns at the feeder or water source while more dominant birds go first.

Another potential hazard in the backyard, especially for birds, is the windows and glass doors in our houses. These can look like open spaces to wildlife, particularly when the sky and trees are reflecting off of them. When birds

or other animals are startled, they just might make a dash for that space. To prevent the resulting injury to the wild creature and the possible damage to your glass, eliminate the reflection with a screen or paper. You might also attach black silhouettes of hawks in flight to the glass, which should give the birds some idea that danger lurks in that direction. It really doesn't matter if the danger they perceive is not the danger that truly awaits them.

INJURED WILDLIFE AND ORPHANS

Occasionally, you will encounter the problem of injured wildlife. There are many well-meaning books on this subject that will present a myriad of methods for caring for this unfortunate creature. But the bottom line is simply this: Caring for any wild creature will require more effort, time, and patience than you can possibly imagine. And except for those trained and experienced in these techniques, the effort will result in failure much more frequently than in success. Finally, laws in many states prohibit the keeping of most wildlife species.

Your best course of action with injured wildlife, and the one that will most often actually benefit the animal, is to confine the creature and contact a veterinarian as quickly as possible. Many vets will be able to recommend the local expert in the care of injured wildlife, someone who is generally experienced and adequately equipped to handle the situation.

With apparently "orphaned" babies, the kindest thing you usually can do is to leave them alone, right where you spotted them. Unless they are in imminent danger from a predator, don't touch the babies, move off some distance (to a concealed location if possible), and wait. Such orphans are usually not lost to their parents. The adult is probably in hiding from you or off finding yet more food for its offspring. Probably it will return soon after you are no longer in sight.

If, on the other hand, you watch for some time and the adult does not come to the youngsters (give it a couple of hours), it may be time to capture and immobilize the babies, and get in touch with a vet or animal rehabilitation expert as mentioned above. If at all possible, maintain a constant watch in hiding and from a distance throughout this period, just in case a cat happens onto the scene.

From time to time you also may be "treated" to uninvited, indoor visits from the wildlife you've encouraged into your backyard. These need not be times of hyperactivity, apprehension, and fear. The animal generally doesn't want to be in your house any more than you want it there. Quietly and casually seal off the room it's in from the rest of the house, open the windows and leave the situation alone for an hour or so. If this occurs at night, also turn off the lights, which may confuse the animal. When you return to the

room, your visitor probably will be gone.

RABIES AND LYME DISEASE

Two of the scariest and most publicized problems associated with wildlife across an increasingly large portion of the continent are rabies and Lyme disease. The principal carriers of both of these dread diseases are wildlife species, which everything you have just read is designed to bring into close proximity to your home, your children, and your pets.

Rabies has lost a great deal of its fear value in the wake of media attention to Lyme disease, but, nonetheless, it continues in surprisingly high numbers in some regions. Rabies is also the easier disease to guard against. Watch for any animal that seems disoriented or acts unusually tame or aggressive. Raccoons, skunks, bats, squirrels, and foxes are especially disposed to this disease, but many

ABOVE and BELOW: Many ornamental plants require special protection from wildlife, especially those species that offer choice food when other, native species are at a low point. Wildlife, too, often needs protective measures, such as guarding birds from collisions with windows.

other species have been recorded. Make sure your children have a thorough understanding of the dangers of such animals, and watch your pets closely to avoid contact.

Your first-choice action is to contact your local animal control authorities for them to remove the animal. If, however, their response is too slow in your consideration and you feel you must take action on your own – something we highly recommend against – wear heavy gloves and clothing in dealing with a suspect animal. The gloves should be destroyed afterward. Get the animal into a safe container with as little contact as possible and take it to a veterinarian immediately for diagnosis. Through all of this, be constantly aware that rabies is spread in the saliva of the infected animal.

Lyme disease, to me, is a much more frightening threat because of its "unseen" nature. It's the only area of my outdoor life where I still employ chemicals, repellents with 100 percent DEET (diethyltoluamide). The Lyme bacterium is spread through the bite of the deer tick (*Ixodes dammini*) in the

Northeast and Midwest, black-legged tick (*I. scapularis*) in the Midwest and Southeast, and western black-legged tick (*I. pacificus*) in the West, creatures so small that they're generally likened to tiny freckles that move. The ticks are carried on various warm-blooded animals and birds, including pets.

Vaccination is now available for pets, but it will probably be several years before it's available for humans. Prevention and early detection are still our best hope. Wear long pants, with socks pulled up over the cuffs, and long-sleeved shirts whenever you travel in weedy or woody areas. The clothing should be light in color to allow

quick detection of any ticks that do grab hold. The DEET repellent should be sprayed across the entire surface of the clothing, with particular attention to cuffs, collar, and socks.

Complete body inspection should follow all outings. Any tick that is found on the body should be removed with tweezers. If the tick is imbedded in the skin, grasp its body with the tweezers *without squashing or squeezing the invader* and pull it back steadily. This will ease out the mouthparts rather than ripping them from the tick. Do not touch the tick with bare hands. Wash the bite area with soap and apply antiseptic.

RIGHT: As wonderful as wildlife in the backyard can be, there will be times when the critters can become a nuisance. Most repeat offenders can be easily caught and removed to a distant wild location in simple live traps, or box traps. The key component of such a trap is a sliding door, which is released by pressure on a trigger plate at the rear of the trap.

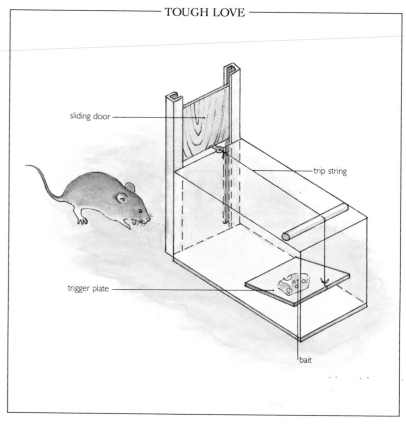

TOUGH LOVE

sliding door

trip string

trigger plate

bait

CONTACTS

American Birding
Association
P.O. Box 6599
Colorado Springs, CO 80934

American Nature Study
Society
5881 Cold Brook Road
Homer, NY 13077

Backyard Wildlife
Association
4920 Liberty Lane
Allentown, PA 18106

Bat Conservation
International
P.O. Box 162603
Austin, TX 78716

Brooks Bird Club Inc.
707 Warwood Avenue
Wheeling, WV 26003

Canadian Nature Federation
453 Sussex Drive
Ottawa, Ontario
Canada K1N 6Z4

Canadian Wildlife
Federation
1673 Carling Avenue
Ottawa, Ontario
Canada K2A 3Z1

Canadian Wildlife Service
Conservation and Protection
Place Vincent Massey
Ottawa, Ontario
Canada K1A 0H3

Cooper Ornithological
Society
Department of Biology
University of California
Los Angeles, CA 90024-1606

Garden Club of America
598 Madison Avenue
New York, NY 10022

Hawk Mountain Sanctuary
Association
Route 2, Box 191
Kempton, PA 19529

International Ecology
Society
1471 Barclay Street
St. Paul, MN 55106-1405

International Society of
Arboriculture
P.O. Box 908
303 West University Avenue
Urbana, IL 61801

Izaak Walton League of
America Inc.
1401 Wilson Boulevard
Level B
Arlington, VA 22209

Laboratory of Ornithology
Cornell University
159 Sapsucker Woods Road
Ithaca, NY 14850

Manomet Bird Observatory
P.O. Box 936
Manomet, MA 02345

Men's Garden Clubs of
America Inc.
5560 Merle Hay Road
Johnston, IA 50131

National Arbor Day
Foundation
100 Arbor Avenue
Nebraska City, NE 68410

National Audubon Society
950 Third Avenue
New York, NY 10022

National Council of State
Garden Clubs Inc.
4401 Magnolia Avenue
St. Louis, MO 63110

National Gardening
Association
180 Flynn Avenue
Burlington, VT 05401

National Institute for
Urban Wildlife
10921 Trotting Ridge Way
Columbia, MD 21044-2831

National Wildflower
Research Center
2600 FM 973 North
Austin, TX 78725

National Wildlife Federation
Urban Wildlife Program
Laurel Ridge Conservation
Education Center
8925 Leesburg Pike
Vienna, VA 22184

National Woodland Owners
Association
374 Maple Avenue East
Suite 204
Vienna, VA 22180

North American Bluebird
Society
P.O. Box 6295
Silver Spring, MD 20906

U.S. Fish & Wildlife Service
Washington, DC 20240

Wildlife Habitat Canada
1704 Carling Avenue
Suite 301
Ottawa, Ontario
Canada K2A 1C7

Wildlife Habitat
Enhancement Council
1010 Wayne Avenue
Suite 1240
Silver Spring, MD 20910

Wildlife Management
Institute
Suite 725
1101 14th Street NW
Washington, DC 20005

Wildlife Society
5410 Grosvenor Lane
Bethesda, MD 20814

BIBLIOGRAPHY

The following books are recommended for anyone wishing additional information on backyard wildlife gardening.

Brainerd, John W. *The Nature Observer's Handbook.* Chester, Conn.: Globe Pequot Press, 1986.

Brown, Tom, Jr. *Tom Brown's Field Guide to the Forgotten Wilderness.* New York: Berkley Publishing Group, 1987.

Druse, Ken. *The Natural Garden.* New York: Clarkson N. Potter, 1988.

Halpin, Ann Moyer. *Foolproof Planting.* Emmaus, Pa.: Rodale Press, 1990.

Harrison, George H. *The Backyard Bird Watcher.* New York: Simon and Schuster, Inc., 1979.

Mahnken, Jan. *Hosting the Birds.* Pownal, Vt.: Storey Communications, 1989.

Merilees, William J. *Attracting Backyard Wildlife.* Stillwater, Minn.: Voyageur Press, 1989.

Mitchell, John Hanson. *A Field Guide to Your Own Back Yard.* New York: W. W. Norton and Company, 1985.

Phillips, Harry R. *Growing and Propagating Wild Flowers.* Chapel Hill, N.C.: University of North Carolina Press, 1985.

Schneck, Marcus. *Butterflies: How to Identify and Attract Them to Your Garden.* Emmaus, Pa.: Rodale Press, 1990.

Smyser, Carol A. *Nature's Design.* Emmaus, Pa.: Rodale Press, 1982.

Terres, John K. *Songbirds in Your Garden.* New York: Harper and Row Publishers, 1987.

INDEX

ACKNOWLEDGMENTS

Quarto Publishing would like to thank the following for supplying pictures for this book:

While every effort has been made to trace and acknowledge all copyright holders we would like to apologize should any omissions have been made.

Key: a=above, b=below, l=left, r=right, c=center

page 2 Mae Scanlan; 8-9 PHOTRI; 10 Rick Marsi; 12 Unicorn Stock Photos/Karen Holsinger Mullen; 13 Gerald L. Wicklund; 14a Marcus Schneck, b Unicorn Stock Photos/James A. Anderson; 15 Unicorn Stock Photos/Gerry Schnieders; 17 Dick Mermon; 18 Marcus Schneck; 19 Unicorn Stock Photos/W. H. Alburty; 21 Scott Weidensaul; 29 Jerry Pavia; 30 Steve Maslowski; 32 Scott Weidensaul; 33 Wildlife Matters; 34 Cleo Freelance Photo; 35 Marcus Schneck; 36 Marcus Schneck; 37 Steve Maslowski; 42 Steve Maslowski; 44 l Allen H. Benton, r Unicorn Stock Photos/Martha McBride; 45 Gregory K. Scott; 46 Scott Weidensaul; 47a Erika Klass, b Richard Day; 49 Marcus Schneck; 50 Steve Maslowski; 51 Unicorn Stock Photos/Mary Stadtfeld; 58 Jim West; 59 Tim Delong;

61 Scott Weidensaul; 62a Mae Scanlan, b Scott Weidensaul; 63 Ro-ma Stock/Robert Marien; 66 Mae Scanlan; 671 Pat Gerlach, r Scott Weidensaul; 72 Cleo Freelance Photo; 73a Mae Scanlan, b Chuck Mann; 75a PHOTRI/Irene Vandermolen, bl Gregory K. Scott, br Unicorn Stock Photos; 76-77 Scott Weidensaul; 76a John Conneely, b Betty Jo Stockton; 78 Karl H. Maslowski; 81 PHOTRI/B. Kulik; 83 Marcus Schneck; 88 Erika Klass; 891 G. E. Robbins, r Richard Day; 91a Richard Day, b Betty Jo Stockton; 92 Steve Maslowski; 93 Steve Maslowski; 94 Marcus Schneck; 95 Steve Maslowski; 98a PHOTRI/Leonard Lee Rue, b Steve Maslowski; 99 Jim West; 1041 Rick Marsi, r Richard Day; 105 Scott Weidensaul; 106 Mae Scanlan; 1071 Marcus Schneck, r Tim Delong; 108 Steve Maslowski; 152 PHOTRI; 153 Karl H. Maslowski; 154 Steve Maslowski; 155a Gregory K. Scott, b Steve Maslowski.

Garden feature photography by:
Scott Weidensaul pages 22-25; Kim Leighton pages 38-41; Gary Svoboda pages 52-55; Rosemary Shelton: Click the Photo Connection pages 68-71; Robert J. Keir pages 84-87; John Haviland pages 100-103